HOW TO MAKE NO FRIENDS EVERYWHERE

BRENT BROCK & JAY WILBURN

Fading Memory Press

How to Make No Friends Everywhere

Edited: Tamara Crow

Cover and Interior Art: Luke Spooner
    www.CarrionHouse.com

Book Layout: Lori Michelle
    www.TheAuthorsAlley.com

TABLE OF CONTENTS

INTRODUCTION:
FEELING THE LIFE DRAIN OUT

I WANT TO leave something more for my kids than money.

Feeling the life leaving my body, and feeling it come back in, has a way of changing your perspective. It did for me, anyway.

I've reconsidered whether to write about all this at least three times since I started the process. The fact that you're reading it now indicates I decided it mattered enough to tell my story as best I could. Making sense of my past is part of it. If it's absolution I'm seeking, I don't know my commitment level. Some level of resolution for my life, and the lives I've touched, is more likely. Forgiving and forgiveness are always a possibility. We try to move the pieces of our lives around to manipulate the outcome. Sometimes it works, but a lot of times we're still trying to fix the broken pieces of our childhood long after we are old.

The biggest reason to write this is to leave a legacy for my children that is measured some way other than dollars and cents. Something that explains why and how my life, and our lives together, played out the way they did. If I can accomplish that to a degree here,

BRENT BROCK & JAY WILBURN

then the way forward for them might make more sense, too.

Not too far from that primary goal is how this might help anyone else who reads it. Going through obstacles, overcoming the odds, or still going through the middle of it is easier, if you know you're not alone. I've exceeded my dreams in many ways, but there are other things, personal things, that are only starting to be good.⟨There is no clean and easy path through life where we get to walk it without getting hurt. ⟩

If I'm not exactly sure what I want from this, I'm sure of what I don't want. I don't want pity. I don't want to compare suffering. In a contest where we see who got hurt the most, or who is the biggest victim, no one wins. Nothing I have gained has ever come to me from wallowing. I tell about my medical issues because they are part of the story, not because I want to make my path look tougher than yours. When I talk about my difficult past and childhood, it is only because that is where the story begins, not where it ends.

If any benefit comes to someone else's life from knowing this story, then it was worth telling.

So, I felt the life drain right out of me.

For a while, I had a problem with water I couldn't seem to clear from my left ear. Every time I stepped out of the shower, I couldn't get it to drain out. Turned out to be the beginning of a brain tumor, and a long twisting path of medical issues that continue in one form or another to this day.

There was one hospital in the state that had access to the Cyberknife developed by the military. It delivered radiation with precision around the tumor, while never hitting the same tissue twice. I was fortunate that my surgeon had transferred to the hospital from the Mayo Clinic before I needed his expertise.

After I got home, I was sick for five days. I had sales calls and I was muscling through. It was August in Atlanta in 2007, which was one of the hottest months in the state on record. On the way home one day, I started feeling dizzy and was nearly blinded. I had to tilt my head to see to stay in my lane.

I got home in one piece, laid down, and proceeded to slowly die.

My first wife and I were having problems. By that, I mostly mean that having to live with me at that point in my life was a problem for anyone. Not the kind of problems where she wanted me to die, but the kind where if I was in a bad mood, it was best to leave me alone. So, she did, and I could have died.

I was getting sick in the downstairs bathroom and I passed out. She found me there on the floor. Turned out the toilet was full of blood. I am colorblind, so this had been going on awhile without my knowing.

She drove me to the hospital, but on the way, I made her pull over. I didn't want to go to the hospital; I wanted a cheeseburger. We sat in the Wendy's parking lot, debating between a cheeseburger and going to the hospital before I died. It's hard to think clearly when you don't have enough blood going through your brain.

I convinced her to take me back home. Even when I'm dying and altered, I'm convincing. Some skills serve us well in some places, but are deadly in others. I passed more blood at home and I finally got to the hospital with no more debate.

It took them too long to find an answer. Doctors came into my room in large committees. I can't even die without having more meetings. Not knowing the answer is an all too common theme in my medical history.

They thought it was cancer for a while, which maybe they shouldn't be blamed for, with my recent surgery. But then we get into a series of blunders and product failures that have plagued me throughout the last several years. And on this occasion, hospital drama and ego trips fit for gods, between doctors and surgeons, nearly cost me everything. I do blame them for that, and still get hot when I have to talk about it to this day.

Eventually, they would discover it was an ulcer in my colon, which was a rare occurrence. By the time they figured it out, it was already perforating. It was supposed to be a laparoscopic surgery, but I woke to find myself cut from my sternum to my crotch. I was stapled up like Frankenstein and wasn't expecting it at all. I was confused.

But, my God, the pain.

I also woke up too soon in recovery. The nurses had to lay on top of me to hold me down. They had to keep me from ripping open my incision. I was screaming from pain more intense than I ever imagined possible. Remembering it now brings me to tears.

One of the nurses got in my face and begged me, "Look at me ... Look at me ... Look at me!"

I was able to focus on her for only a second.

"You have to stop. You have to. You're scaring the other patients. You have to stop ..."

She was on my left. I raised my eyes from her face back to the ceiling. There was no way I could *not* scream. There was so much pain.

One of the nurses yelled, "Give him something. Knock him out."

I recall another saying, "I can't give him any more. It'll kill him."

On the way to my room, my mother saw me. I mumbled something. Her first words were, "Why is he awake?"

Later, in the room, she begged them to help my pain, to help her son.

The floor nurse said, "I'll get him comfortable. I've been doing this a long time. If it takes me all night, I'll get him comfortable."

All this happened because life came back into me. One hell of a welcome back into the world.

My epiphany about life came before this, when they were still trying to figure out what was wrong.

Before the surgery, I was losing blood in unpredictable ways, so they were running out of my blood type and struggling to get more in time. I might have had as many as nine transfusions at that time.

It may have been during a shift change, but at some point, they fell behind. They strapped me to the table and tilted my head toward the floor. I didn't even know those beds did that. I'm not sure the angle, but my head was almost at floor level as they tried anything they could to keep blood pressure in my heart and brain.

I didn't know if I was ever coming out of that hospital. I felt the life leaving me. I felt death. I had passed out before. I had done that recently. Death feels different. It was not a thing I could hold or explain, but I would describe it best as life retreating, creating an absence. And life was vacating me in that moment. The void expanded from the inside out and was taking me with it.

As I faded, it became okay. It wasn't okay. It wasn't right. But it just had to be. I had no control over passing or staying. If my time was up, hanging upside down as they tried to catch up on blood, there was nothing I could do about it in that moment. A lot of things didn't matter anymore in that instant, where everything was okay and not okay at once.

I was gone.

But then I could feel the life coming back into me. Everything became possible again because life came back. I had experienced that moment when priorities in life shrink down with the closing of life and the growing of the void.

I believe in God and I believe in an afterlife. That does not change the reality of the limited time we have on Earth to do good by the people we love, or to leave collateral damage all around our path. It does not change the fact that we leave some kind of legacy, positive or negative, once we are gone.

Ego trips, drama, anger, and violence leave lasting legacies long after us. I believe kindness, grace, mercy, and love do, too. You can be a great success on either path. You can earn money either way. You can build a reputation and have friends with either legacy. But you can't take both paths at once and only one is a worthy path, no matter how much money or success you leave behind. There is either light or shadow left after us, and it matters a great deal which kind of legacy we leave.

Successes and failures pile up behind both paths. Legacy is what we build that lasts beyond those successes and failures. In that regard, it is the most important thing we build, with whatever life we have left.

Starting now.

After that moment of tasting death, I still had the surprise of waking up too soon and screaming in pain ahead of me. These new realizations did not save my first marriage. It did not cure me from anger. It didn't guarantee that I might not end up drinking again. The path to being okay was only beginning.

But you have to begin somewhere, so let's move on to the next chapter, and back to the beginning.

CHAPTER 1:

NOWHERE HE COULDN'T FIND US

MY FATHER LITERALLY died under a sign that read: Abused alcohol since age 12.

By my estimation, that might have been the only marker he ever really earned.

He was attached to all kinds of tubes and hoses in the hospital bed, all yellow and swollen from kidney failure. The last words he said to me as I was leaving his hospital room were, "I'll be out of here next week. I'll call you. Let's take your sister's new boyfriend fishing."

I suspected that would be the last time I saw him alive, and that was fine by me.

With him talking about fishing like we were old buddies, it wasn't lost on me how many times my mother and I tried to run away from him and failed. If she wasn't as tough as she was, I'm certain he would have killed her on any of a number of occasions. She had more toughness in her little finger than he had in his whole body, and in the end, we all outlived him.

In the 1960s, he and my Papaw, my dad's father, had taken a trip to Michigan and that's where my father met my mother, working in a factory. She went to Catholic School. He brought her back to the hills of southeastern Kentucky and she had to adapt in a hurry.

My mother and I tried to make our escape from him a number of times, without success. We were tracked down and forced to return with him and his posse every time.

In the middle of the night, I would wake up with a hand over my mouth.

"Shhh! We're leaving. Let's go."

We'd go out the back and down a hill into a waiting car. And we were off into the night.

A few days later, I would be discovered hiding in my cousin's closet in the next town over. Below the anger, you could see the sense of dark satisfaction on his face. There was nowhere we could go that he couldn't reach. Nowhere to hide that he wouldn't think to check. We never went quite far enough to get away completely for a long time. The Hills and a badge had a long reach in that small world of Harlan, Kentucky—Bloody Harlan.

But Carl Brock died at age 49 because a badge and all the guns in the world won't save a man like that forever. It was fall of 1991, and I had recently graduated from high school.

In a way, he never died, because he still haunts me. He haunts me from the side. Never more than a step or two to one side or the other. If I ever stray just a step or two off the path, he's there to possess me. I hear him in unkind words I'm trying to kill before they escape my lips to become verbal or emotional abuse. He's there to show me how to be an angry drunk, if I ever care to try that on for size. He's there to whisper violent solutions into my ear, for any and every problem. Because of him, I entered the ring at age two or three, ready to fight any challenger for any offense, and I'm not sure I ever stepped back out.

Any man who measures his father to be worthy of hating or fearing, has to worry about becoming him one day. Maybe there is nowhere I can hide that his ghost can't find me, either.

Harlan County, Kentucky is a dry county. It was when I lived there, and still is today. Frozen in time. Many people think of dry counties as meaning you can't buy or sell alcohol there. With Harlan, it also meant you couldn't possess it or drink it, either. Or you weren't supposed to.

My father was a cop and a bootlegger. Yet, somehow, we stayed poor all the time.

Our house and property sat on a wide spot in the road. That road being Straight Creek, which was named as a bit of a joke because there weren't ten straight feet on any stretch of Straight Creek. It wound through the rolling potato hills, which gave way to Appalachian hills and, eventually, the mountains proper. That is Appalachia, hanging onto wide spots in the road.

Mamaw and Papaw, my father's parents, lived in a single-wide trailer on the other side of the railroad tracks that split the property. Henry and Tisha Brock. Although, it wasn't until I read her obituary that I realized her name wasn't Tishy, like I and everyone I ever knew called her. They sometimes called me "Little Carl," but meant no insult by it. They were born, him in 1908 and her in 1910, with multiple generations of our family, in those hills.

HOW TO MAKE NO FRIENDS EVERYWHERE

My papaw worked the coal mines in Harlan when he was in his 20s and 30s, back in the 1940s. He would draw a black lung check until the day he died. I saw an old pay stub of his that read 25 cents an hour. My cousin, Larry Brock, was injured in a mining accident much later in the 1960s and broke his back. My father tooled around with the mines for a time, but not as much as others in the family. Coal mining, coal trucks, and criminal activity were about all the money-making action that was going on there for generations.

The house my family lived in on our side of that wide spot was a squared circle. The living room connected to the kitchen (or whatever we were using it for at the time). The kitchen connected to my sisters' room. Their room connected to my parents' room, where I slept in a crib at the end of their bed. Then, back around to the living room. I sometimes rode my tricycle around that connection, with a friend, over and over until our parents yelled at us to find something else to do.

There was a little well-house. The pump sometimes worked and often didn't, but was always full of sulfur. The sinks, tub, and toilet that connected to the well were always stained. We had to draw water from the creek and wash our clothes there.

There was technology in the 1970s, but I was aware of none of it. I didn't see a bicycle until I left Kentucky. My papaw told me about the first airplane he ever saw freaking him out. I didn't see my first black person until later, either. We were poor and isolated.

I tried never to miss school because that was my only reliable meal.

My father enjoyed a great deal of impunity with his badge. To exploit the market for booze in Harlan, he would take my mom, and sometimes me, over county lines to either Hazard or Corbin. They would load cases of beer, wine, and liquor in the car, depending on what the customers wanted. They had it stashed in the coal piles and everywhere. He'd also bust his competition and resell what contraband he took from them. I had my first drink at maybe two or three. My father gave me a snub nosed .38 for my fifth birthday.

He was never without multiple weapons on or near his person. Never. Even when he was a patient at the hospital, he was always packing. I was in my first drive-by shooting with him when I was six.

He ran illegal gambling out of the pool hall. I spent most of my days standing on a chair shooting pool. He'd sometimes bet grown men that I could beat them, and I did. I remember one particular day I lost him what I thought was all the money we had. We did without, because I lost. That's how my dad saw it. Not that he had gambled away the money.

On the day of the shooting, some men were angry at my father over a gambling debt. He pushed me to the floor of the car and returned fire. I saw him shoot at people on multiple occasions. He even shot at me once, but if there is any credit to extend to him on something like this, he wasn't aiming at me.

I remember when I was five, going to sleep in my bed and waking up in my grandparents' trailer. I looked down the hill and saw our house was gone, replaced by ashes. My father was away on a fishing trip and my mom said, "The house caught fire and burned down."

Even at that age, the first words out of my mouth were, "You guys did it."

They had somehow gotten me up the hill without waking me up, and proceeded to commit arson for insurance fraud.

My dad went on to build a boarding house that wouldn't have passed any inspection, not even in those hills, but no inspectors got around to driving up the bends of that winding road. He rented rooms to two truckers, Danny and Trenton. That turned into a whole different problem that we'll unpack some in the next chapter.

I helped, as much as a kid my age could, with the construction of the outhouse facilities for my dad's backroom business. Very poorly constructed, at the top of some rickety stairs, on the side of a hill in the woods.

We also built a cinderblock room on the back of a trailer he called the bear house. Years later, my dad would cut the wall out of the trailer and make that backroom part of the house. He lived in that very trailer until the day he died in that University of Kentucky Hospital bed in Lexington, under the "Abused alcohol since age 12" sign, on the spot where I wished him dead.

He was the nicest guy certain people ever met, and the most dangerous I could imagine. And he haunts me from the side as I struggle to not become him. He was an angry drunk, and a mean sober sometimes, too.

We tried more than once to escape him, and failed. We never succeeded until we made it to Louisiana. My sisters wouldn't escape until later. And then, there was more escaping to be done after that.

CHAPTER 2:

ALWAYS PLAYING CATCH-UP ON MY LIFE

THE FIRST THING I ever learned in school, the first thing I remember learning, was that the year we escaped to Louisiana, it was 1979. I was eight years old.

My father once chased us to the next town over, in Kentucky. He pounded on the side of the trailer where we were. He yelled he was going to kill me if I hid from him, and I pissed myself at the sound of his voice. I did hide in a closet. He did find me, and I was sure that was the end of my life. But we lived to get away, finally. My sisters, as I said, would take longer to escape.

When my father built the boarding house over the ashes of our old house, he rented rooms to a couple of coal truckers, Danny and Trenton. They were both about seventeen or eighteen at the time. They were chemically dependent, so they fit right in.

Laura and Lisa, my sisters, were about thirteen and fourteen, and Laura turned up pregnant. My father stabbed Danny over it. They left and got married. Not long after that, Lisa got pregnant, too, and moved up the road to live with Trenton, on his family's property. That was their way to escape, at first. And like my mother and I, they hadn't yet escaped far.

The last clear and joyful memory I have of both my sisters and I all together was down at the swimming hole back in the Kentucky hills. My mother would take us. Sometimes my father was there, too, back when we were still little and all still living together. Going to the swimming hole down the creek a piece was pure and actual fun. We have all had fun since. We have enjoyed time together in pairs. We've all been together in the same place at times since. But that was the last meeting spot where everything was joy for us together as a trio.

Mom and I made it to Lafayette, Louisiana and landed in a single-wide trailer with my Uncle George, Sr. and Aunt Tina. They had two kids, my cousin George Junior, a year younger than me, and his sister Tammy, a couple years younger. Tracking time is tricky when you're a kid, but a few weeks or maybe a few months later, Laura left Danny and brought her daughter Christina with her to stay with us in that same single-wide.

It was the nicest place I had ever lived.

My cousin George had Star Wars figures and we played with those. They had a TV with multiple channels, with more picture than snow. Between the trailers, they had a plastic kiddie pool they filled with water. I got my first bicycle. I'd never even seen one before. I started late, so I had training wheels longer than anyone else around; I had to play catch-up. But it was the best life I could imagine.

That trailer park was situated on both sides of the two-lane road near a 7-11 convenience store. There was no rhyme or reason to the lots. A few nicer trailers were on graded lots, but most were just stuck wherever there was space between the others. We'd go up to that 7-11 to play video games or steal candy.

I don't know the circumstances, but I ended up getting sent back to Kentucky for a short period of time and I stayed with my sister Lisa, her husband Trenton, and their daughter Brandy, on land they shared with Trenton's mother Roberta.

I went back to my same grade school I left. The school sat at the end of that road called "The Head of the Creek." Straight Creek led out past all our houses and split into a Y fork. One arm of that fork ascended over Pine Mountain, through a dangerous stretch of turtle hills, to where Harlan proper sat on the other side. Runoff came down and eroded the slope around the road, making the drive jagged and treacherous. Trucks ran off it from time to time.

The school didn't know what to do with me. None of the schools I bounced through knew what to do. I was tested and tested again, over the years. My irregular education and unconventional upbringing led to me scoring really high in some areas and remedial in others. That did not paint a clear picture for educators to handle me in the 70s, 80s, and early 90s. I got placed in third grade, they moved me to fifth, and then back to third in one school year.

First time I ever picked up a bat was during that second, and final, stint in Kentucky. I was terrible. I couldn't hit the ball. I lacked athletic ability in most every sport I tried, until I discovered wrestling. I guess if the sport involved fighting, I was well prepared to take it on.

My father made an appearance on occasions. He had made me piss myself in a closet at one point, but then he brought me a little Suzuki 50, a kid's motorcycle, for a gift. He was showing off, doing little donuts on the gravel road of Trenton's family property. These gravels were huge, like small boulders. My dad was riding this motorbike made for kids and only wearing shorts and flip flops. He wiped out and ate it, bad. It absolutely tore him up.

Grocery stores out there were third-world. They built up makeshift cinderblock buildings on concrete floors and just hung out a shingle. Everyone out there was on one government program or another, from poverty assistance to checks for black lung. Some got very good at finding ways to get more than one check. Everyone operated on credit. Not credit cards, but accounts with the storeowners. They kept their books of debt, same as my dad kept his books of gamblers' shortfalls. When they got their checks, they settled up. If they ran up too much debt, they got cut off and had to find supplies somewhere else.

People would bring old clothes up for the poor people in the hills. We'd go to a barn full of clothes and pick out whatever we could find to wear from the piles. They would be ten cents a piece and, back when my mother still lived there, she would take out the money from her coin purse to buy what she could.

My sister Lisa didn't get to go out much. I remember she once got to go to an REO Speedwagon concert with Trenton. They came back after having a few and blasted REO Speedwagon from the radio. She had gotten a shirt from the concert and was so happy.

I went back to Louisiana. She escaped with

Brandy a few years later and joined us, once life with Trenton got to be too much. Trenton's family would then kidnap Brandy directly from her bus stop one morning.

My mother met my stepdad in Louisiana. It was a whirlwind romance and they were married within a couple months. We moved into his trailer over in Duson, about 15 miles from that trailer park in Lafayette. He provided stability, was loving to her and me, caring, kind, supportive, and they have been married ever since. He went by Junior and I called him Junior forever before I finally called him Dad. Wish I had started calling him Dad much sooner.

Junior had eleven siblings. The oldest was William, who we called Uncle Bill. My step-father worked hard, and always looked for legitimate work. William was a hustler, a conman, and a criminal. He stood by his family, but that was the trade he gravitated toward and he taught his brothers how to do it, too. Junior trended away from that sort of thing, but he idolized William and would join in on anything his older brother told him to. Junior spent some time in prison for it, but that sort of thing was outside his core nature, while it was firmly in William's wheelhouse.

Junior idolized William and doted on him. He set the man upon a pedestal and everyone saw William as the guy you went to when you needed something no one else could get done. Uncle Bill skirted the rules with style, and some measure of success.

As a result, I got two messages from my stepdad. One was intentional; the other wasn't. Junior taught me directly to work hard, even when life is tough, and obstacles are high. He indirectly taught me that men like William, skilled in criminal activity, were to be admired and aspired after. My admiration of Junior and his admiration of William, left an impression. I took both lessons to heart throughout my youth.

Uncle Bill died of a heart attack in 1996 while washing his truck. He was still the man you went to when you needed someone with special skills.

I got a paper route. The newspapers were delivered to one location. I picked them up and rubberbanded them. If it was raining, I bagged them, too. My parents would sometimes help when it rained, but it was my job, and the work was left to me. I learned to balance my bike and delivered the papers. I kept a couple extra, so if anyone called and claimed they hadn't gotten a paper, I rolled another one and rode over again to deliver it.

Collections were on me, too. If someone was late paying, that came out of my money. My parents didn't help with that, either. So, I was going to grown adults, late on their payments, on my own, to collect the money. Working the route was me living up to the example of Junior. Working collections was more like living up to Uncle Bill. Maybe with a touch of Carl Brock, with his badge and his book of gamblers with outstanding debts.

The first birthday party I ever had in my life was in Louisiana. My cousin George was a year and a month younger than me, so the family decided to have our parties together. We had it at McDonald's. We both invited everyone from our classes. All of George's class showed up. One kid from my class showed up. The present from that kid was the first gift

I ever had from anyone outside of my family. I wasn't thankful, though. I would have rather'd no one show up than just one.

I changed schools multiple times in Louisiana, before changing schools several times in other states, as I got into higher grades. It was hard to get a footing anywhere, or with anyone. We moved from the trailer, to an apartment, and later to a house behind a carpet store owned by a guy named Gyro, who drove a fancy sports car.

While we were still in the trailer in Duson, my mom was working nights at a nursing home, cleaning bedpans and such. She had to wear white shoes with steel toes that hurt her feet, but she had been doing "steel-toed" work from all the way back when she was single, working in factories in Detroit.

She was sleeping in the early afternoon and it was hot as hell. We didn't have a kiddie pool like we had 15 miles over in Lafayette, at Uncle George and Aunt Tina's. I missed that pool. I wanted her to take me, but I couldn't get her woken up, more than half awake, long enough for a straight answer. And she wouldn't agree to take me.

I was still maybe 8 or 9 at the time, and had just gotten my training wheels off. I got on my bike and rode the whole way. For some reason, I didn't think to put on shoes and grew to regret it, but was too stubborn to admit defeat and go back. I curled my toes over the pedals because they were spiked to grip the soles of your shoes. I pedaled with my curled toes on the unspiked sides, with my heels up, for 15 miles. My foot would slip, especially after I grew tired, and spike the arch of my bare foot. I kept going, though, through the heat and stop signs and all the turns. I should have gotten lost, but I made it.

Dropping my bike, I staggered over to the pool and fell in. No one was even home at the trailer, so I couldn't get in. I just played in that pool until, hours later, the adults arrived and found me.

Everyone was angry and concerned. I was confused. I was confused a lot, but this time I was road-weary and hurt on top of it.

I channeled Uncle Bill and Big Carl to put together my cover story. My mom had been half awake, so I claimed that I said to her, "I want to ride my bike to the pool."

"What? ... What?" my mother said, groggy and completely plausible in my imaginary script.

"I'm going to ride my bike there."

"Okay, fine. Whatever. Just let me sleep."

With my most indignant rebuttal, to the adults over me, "I had permission."

And, performance complete, I take my bow. I got skilled at talking my way out of the trouble I made for myself.

Another time, while we were still in that Lafayette trailer park, we stole some candy from the 7-11. There was a fireworks stand down the road that was seasonal. I broke the lock on it, and we got inside. The shelves were clear, so we put our candy out, opened up the front, and started selling our stolen candy. It was just like a wide spot makeshift grocery off of Straight Creek in the hills of Kentucky.

It turned out it was time for the fireworks shop to open up again, so they pulled up and found us there minding the store. Instead of freaking out like would probably happen today, they started talking to us.

"Looks like you got a business going here."

"We do."

"How about we make a trade?"

They pulled out a gross of bottle rockets. When you have a package that big, they are wrapped in plastic. The rockets are crammed side by side on both ends of the block.

"What do you say, kids?"

The candy we had wasn't even worth a fraction of a gross of fireworks. We agreed.

"No, just leave all the candy on the shelves. Don't move any of it. We'll set up in here. You can just take the fireworks and go play."

We fired them off at each other and had our own drawn-out wars. We would team up in groups of two or three. Then, it was open season.

One day, a rocket went astray under some guy's car and exploded. The guy got upset and our dads, George Sr. and Junior, were made to get involved. The guy was adamant his vehicle was damaged by the rocket and he demanded a new paint job.

"They're kids. Your car is fine."

The argument continued.

My stepdad summed it up by saying, "I'm not giving you any money. We can fight about it, if you'd like. If it'll make you feel better, let's fight."

The guy left with no money and no fight.

Bottle Rocket War was a war of attrition and though we were heavily armed, we ran through our rockets in short order. No one lost an eye or a finger, by some miracle, so peace was restored again, if not order. We'd always find money for more ammo, eventually.

We came out ahead on that hustle.

So, Trenton's family came to Louisiana after Lisa had fled and they snatched Brandy up from the bus stop to take her back to Kentucky. Now why did they do that?

Logic breaks down fast in family disputes anyway. When you add in hotheaded, high, and criminally-prone individuals to the mix, it all stops making sense even faster. If someone like Carl Brock has his fingers in it, all bets are off.

Why was my father willing to kill us for running away one day, but didn't care anymore later? The stories vary and conflict on what happened when we left Kentucky for Lafayette. Why was I sent back again? And if Trenton's family, and dear old Roberta, cared so much about Brandy that they were willing to kidnap her to have her back, then why hold her for ransom?

I was a kid and not included in on the details, other than the usual way adults forget kids are in the room when they are arguing about adult stuff within earshot. My sister was beside herself with rage and fear, obviously. Hard to argue that leaving Trenton was the wrong choice at that point.

My mother handled negotiations. I don't know what they wanted. I don't know what was agreed to. But for a group willing to kidnap a child to have her back, some agreement was made to return her. They got something. Whatever it was, it was worth more to them than Brandy, and that was the end of it. On that count, it doesn't matter what it was because they bargained over a child's life and that shows their worth as human beings.

Like I said, logic breaks down when you're dealing with family and hate. It's not about what it is supposed to be about anymore. None of it makes sense the way love and kindness are supposed to make sense. Life doesn't make sense until you learn to operate on something other than hate, anger, fear, and ignorance.

So, I was confused as a kid, and confused as I grew older, in many different places. Always confused. Always off balance. Always playing catch-up. Trying to catch-up with my own life. For much of my life, I operated from a position of disadvantage. Most of that was outside my control. Other trouble was of my own making. I felt disadvantaged for my accent, my hygiene, my poverty, my developmental delays, and my knowledge about the world.

I could still be working from a place of disadvantage today, if I chose to. I could make a case for being a victim of circumstances, if that were my goal. Nothing of worth is down that path, though. No ransom worth negotiating my life over lies there. That's not where success is found.

I carry this past with me. It defines me in the way our past has to. I don't want it to define my future and my destiny, anymore, though. Knowing it and owning it frees me up to redefine myself. I can push back from the half of me that represents the ghosts of Uncle Bill and my bootlegger father. I can work toward the part of me that represents the best parts of Junior. I can work beyond him to be the better version of myself I should be. I can strive to be better than the ghosts that haunt me and not make, or continue to make, the same mistakes they did.

HOW TO MAKE NO FRIENDS EVERYWHERE

I've felt more than once like I'm still pedaling a bike from one trailer park to another with no shoes. My feet hurt and it's hot. There are more turns along the journey than I track and I'm exhausted. Even the goal can sometimes feel hardly worth it.

But there's still something beyond our goals and successes, too. Something bigger than the journey itself. We are leaving an impression on the world and those around us by what we do, how we struggle, and what we admire. That legacy means something bigger than ourselves, and that defines who we are and who we need to be.

There were a lot more turns along my journey, once we found our way out of Louisiana.

CHAPTER 3:

ATTRACTED TO THE CHAOS THAT DESTROYS ME

My FATHER, CARL BROCK, gave the go-ahead for the kidnapping of my niece, Brandy. My best guess is that my mother was dealing with him when she was negotiating for the girl's release. If that is true, then I believe making my mother seek his permission to have Brandy back was more reward for him than whatever ransom they ultimately agreed to.

When I visited him once, later in life, he told me he had come after us in Louisiana. He brought his posse, just like all the other times, he claimed. And he sent those men to kill my mother and my stepdad, Junior. In his version of reality, he called it off at the last moment, afraid that I might be caught in the crossfire.

Junior didn't have a gun and never did, other than a couple he bought me over the years because I liked them, and a couple he obtained and then pawned for extra money to get us by. Carl carried an arsenal with him everywhere he went, and he assumed everyone else was as paranoid, armed, and potentially dangerous as himself.

I don't know what portion of Carl Brock's stories

are true. I'm not sure how many of his lies he believed, himself, and how many he just wished were true.

Knowing the man mostly from the pieces of his soul I carry around trapped inside myself, I think he desperately wanted the story of the near-assassination and another attempted kidnapping to be true. He needed it to be true, and he needed me to believe it. Carl Brock could never admit he surrendered. It can't be true that he lost my mother to another man, because Carl was less than a man in all the ways that matter to a wife and a son. Or that Junior was the man we needed because he had those missing pieces. Carl Brock needed the reality of my mother and Junior being alive and well to be his idea. The god he wanted to believe he was, when he put on his badge and enforced his will upon the Kentucky hills of his sovereign domain, could only tolerate my mother and Junior being happy together, if it was something he granted them by calling off Death himself. And he needed me to believe that my freedom, and everything I accomplished without him, was a gift he granted me by his benevolence. But I had to believe he could have taken it all away.

By his permission. To this day, I hate seeking permission from anyone, for anything.

Sometimes I feel only partially convinced the real world is as real as we think it is. Sometimes it only seems real because I need it to be. Other times, reality is so intense and clear it is excruciating. I often felt like I had to push things that were too real away from me.

Carl Brock was a man driven by hate, vengeance, anger, and darkness. He was the kind of man that seemed to be seeking vengeance for the day he was born. It bothered him that no one asked his permission in the matter. In reality, these were the gifts he granted me. This was the shadow he left in place of a legacy. I have come to believe these things are not just under the surface for me. They are my surface. They are my defaults, if I do not consciously choose to go another way. They are my impulse and my instinct, if I do not choose to follow reason and my better angels. Kindness, mercy, forgiveness, and love are available to me, but I have to choose them. I have to work for them because the gifts of my father, the Kentucky god of chaos, are easier to access, if I don't choose differently.

My family, Junior's family, had the spirit of the gypsy caravan. They moved with the work. Louisiana had experienced an oil boom, which had created construction demand, which was why our lives intersected his when they did. In '84, the oil business dried up for a while and a housing crisis followed. Even as a kid, I knew something was wrong. I could see abandoned buildings and entire neighborhoods for sale, sometimes. I recognized the look of death and chaos.

We moved on to Florida, to follow work there. Junior and William drove up to Jacksonville for work while we lived out in the sticks. Much of my extended family ended up split between South Georgia and Michigan.

We moved on to Colorado after that. All our family, two boxer dogs, two vans, and another compact car formed our caravan across the country.

My clearest memory from that trip is William's

perpetual relaxation. He would lay in his underwear, eating summer sausage off his chest. If anyone needed a meeting with Uncle Bill, they had to go hold court with him there in his underwear in his motel room. He was the guy who could get things done for people, but in the meantime, he wanted to be catered to there on his motel bed.

Denver represented one hard winter for us. Work was scarce. William had a few hustles going, but lived in a house with no heat. My parents and I stayed with one of my mom's friends. They were upper middle class. When I stayed a long weekend with Uncle Bill and his family in their cold, rundown house, I felt more at home there than in the nice house.

I remember one weekend, the family we stayed with in Denver took us up into the Rockies. It was beautiful. That was a great day.

We moved on to Georgia for the same reason we moved anywhere—chasing work. We ended up in a rent-by-the-week motel and we were broke. Uncle Bill left for a while to run a scheme up in Michigan. Not sure what he did, but he came back after a week and a half, flush with cash.

We moved into an apartment with no furniture and used the money we had to buy a few essentials. We got sleeping bags, cookware, and such. We had a TV that sat on a box and I watched the Challenger Space Shuttle explode on that set.

My parents never owned a house until after I was out of high school. Before that, we lived in three houses we rented, as well as apartments and trailers. Always a temporary life. Always momentary stops on the caravan.

For middle school, in the Atlanta area, I ended up in a school with a lot of rich kids. It was very much the haves and have-nots. I gravitated quietly toward kids like myself. I met a close friend whose mom cleaned houses like my mom did. And then connected to others like him. A few rich kids ran with us from time to time as we caused trouble. I never connected to them. The children of CEOs lived lives outside my experience and comfort zone.

I gave the appearance to adults in my life that I was quiet and had no friends. I signed up for nothing, joined nothing, and did no projects. Kids made fun of me for being a have-not. Kids made fun of me when I colored the grass brown and the sky purple without realizing it. Then, I realized certain shades of color were just slightly outside my grasp, too.

Things went well as I began high school and it made me want to run. We had never stayed anywhere as long as we had stayed in Georgia. Warmth, comfort, and stability made me feel like I was being choked by hands I couldn't see. Cold, trouble, and chaos felt more like home, even as it destroyed me from the inside out.

It was one long panic attack, in the midst of the first real calm in my life, which I had no capacity to understand or absorb. I had been trained to handle a world where the gods looked and behaved like Carl Brock. I didn't know what to do in a universe where God offers peace, love, and joy. Not yet.

I was on the football team and being accepted by the popular kids. I sold them pot. I wasn't smoking it. I didn't even need the money. I just wanted their friendship and I wanted to be the guy who could get them things. Maybe I wanted to be like William was in the eyes of my stepdad—just with pants on.

I got the pot from my Uncle Kevin. He rolled it for me because I didn't know how. He told me what I could get for it and then I sold it to my friends in the bathroom.

Everything was going fine and better than ever, but that wasn't fine with me.

I remember walking down the hall of the school as the ongoing panic attack finally boiled over. Everyone's face stood out to me in excruciating reality. I felt like I was a machine, analyzing every detail about them in a detached way that made me feel crazy. I didn't want to see them anymore. I didn't want it to be real.

My cousin George, whose family had moved to the Atlanta area, too, dropped out of school to do flooring with his dad. They lived in the Berkmar school district, so I moved from the North Springs district to there. Right away, I felt unwelcome and that I didn't belong in those halls, either. I felt no connection to any animate or inanimate objects. Nothing. I had friendships and potential at my first high school, but that hadn't been good enough for me, either.

My parents moved to Gwinnett County for my sake. With their new house, I tried going to Central Gwinnett High School. I got a parking permit, even though I wasn't supposed to be eligible as a Sophomore. I lasted around three to five weeks and dropped out of school entirely.

I worked at the movie theater for several months. I didn't want to go back to school at all. I escaped into movies. We would hang out in projection. We'd hang out after closing and just watch movies. One of my friends there had an 8 mm camera and we started making our own movies. He did top-ten lists about things going on in theater and made a breakroom newsletter with staff gossip and other things. He and I clicked, partly because we were both high school dropouts.

I would have never gone back to school if it wasn't for my mother. We were living on an old property with an old house and a barn. We called it the "Farm House." It reminded me a lot of Kentucky. I was feeling empty inside. I was in flight mode still. I was drowning. I slept on a mattress on the floor and my mother woke me up one morning because she was crying about me. She begged me to go back to school.

A couple friends of mine from back in middle school were at Meadowcreek High School, in Gwinnett County, Georgia, by then. I can't remember what they said about school, but what I heard was that it was great for them and I thought I would like it.

My sister, Laura, and her new husband had moved to Georgia and lived in the Meadowcreek district. I used her address and drove myself across the county to Meadowcreek.

After I was back in high school, they had a night school/ alternative school program there that allowed me to go to school and still work during the day for a while. It allowed me to catch up on what I had missed in about five weeks and graduate on time with the class I started high school with.

Even through all those years of moving, I was always dating someone. I started dating a girl at Meadowcreek, but I never let people know where I lived, not even her. I was embarrassed of where and how I lived, and I didn't want word to get around I was out of district. I dodged the question and rejected her requests to see my house and to meet my family.

That didn't last.

I had a desire to keep a low profile. I started wrestling at Meadowcreek, which was a sport that fit my mentality and my informal life training. I also started dating Renee. This was a combination of choices that propelled me into the forefront faster than I was ready, and blew my plan at staying low profile. It was what I always secretly wanted, but not at the rate and magnitude it occurred. When you feel at home in chaos, getting what you want can drive you crazy.

I didn't even really like her, at first. She and a friend of mine were in a phase of horse playing and flirting to see if they were interested in each other. I remember thinking, what does he see in her? I would find out soon enough.

She and I got serious. I was more open and emotionally intimate with her, to the extent that I could be, more than with anyone before her. We were voted cutest couple. I was involved in theater and was voted most likely to end up on Broadway. We ended up getting engaged.

My junior year, Renee was an assistant to one of the English teachers, Mr. Feldman. I had a friend who was taking his class and was concerned about an upcoming test. I wasn't even taking the class, but I got Renee to steal me a copy of the answers. I wanted to be the guy who could get you things.

This guy and his friends were no good at staying

quiet, so everyone found out they had the answers and word got back around to the teacher. Mr. Feldman asked who had the answers ahead of time and this guy raises his hand. When they got him to the office, he ratted me out.

I wanted to protect Renee, so I said I got the answers on my own. I had to cobble together a plausible story for how I pulled it off.

Mr. Smith, the principal, was looking for a way to get through to me. He asked me, "How would your parents feel if they found out you weren't able to go to prom?"

Prom was coming up and, of course, I was planning to take Renee. My parents wouldn't have any idea what I was doing.

But I went with, "They would be very upset with me." I managed to keep a straight face. "They would be hurt."

I got off with not much more punishment than a "talking to" and I went to prom.

Mr. Feldman and I later became friends. He was at my first wedding.

Renee and I were always arguing. I made her feel guilty about things that I had no business pushing onto her. I was great at getting the worst out of people.

I had a friend I hung with and drank with. His father worked mapping cables on a computer for a utility company. He sat in a dark room in his house, working on a computer at all hours. And he drank a lot. There were beer cans everywhere. We all drank together, too.

One Sunday, we were out of beer and we all

decided to make a road trip to Chattanooga to get more beer because you were allowed to buy it there on Sundays. We were drunk when we left and came back with more.

I was really in a bad place and very drunk. I had told my mother not to tell anyone where I was, but she showed up with Renee. For many years, I blamed my mother for what happened next.

Renee and I were screaming at each other. I demanded the ring back and she threw it at me. And that was it.

I would be engaged four times in my life. After Renee, I was briefly engaged to a girl I dated after her, Beth. Then, I've been married twice, both wonderful women with wonderful kids. I'm in the process of trying to be a better man, a better husband this time around, and a better father.

I held out hope for a long time that Renee and I would get back together and stay together.

I reached out more than once to say I was sorry and to try to get Renee back. One time I was mumbling some nonsense to her on the phone. I started telling her about problems I was having. She said, "I heard you got a new girlfriend named Beth. I'm sure she can help you with that."

That broke my heart.

The chorus teacher at Meadowcreek had a 24-year-old brother. She arranged for him and Renee to be in the same place more than once, until they started dating. Highly inappropriate, I thought, and he was my competition. Renee went back and forth between us, over time.

Renee ended up pregnant by him and left him. I

was there to swoop in for her to talk to about it. She said both of us, me and him, got angry, got in fights with her, and made her feel terrible. She said the difference between us was that I would at least bring her roses afterward. I would try.

I thought this meant that I had a chance with her, but I didn't. It was over.

All told, I dropped out of high school and college a total of four times before I graduated from both: high school in 1991 and from college in 1998. Two times I had to catch up on credits to graduate "on time" with the class I started with, at my final high school and final college.

My tendency in life has been to try to push away stable things. That included my relationships. I'm miserable once they are gone, but I've spent my whole life escaping danger, so now part of me wants to escape safety, too. I was quick to anger, and I still can be. When I got into flight mode, I started pushing, so that people would leave me, and I could fall back into the chaos that feels an awful lot like home to a guy who spent most of his formative years in caravans and temporary homes. I'm on the mend, and I'm committed to doing things differently this time around.

I don't need my parents to take any responsibility for any of this. They did the best they could for me, without the best teachers or role models in their lives. My mother fought for me at the most important moments in my life, from fleeing in the night to begging me back into high school. Junior became the dad I needed, even if it took me a long time to call him that.

I accept full responsibility for my life, my choices, and myself. I accept the damage I have caused, and seek to set it right.

Some of the friends I've mentioned in passing in this chapter are still my closest friends in life, even as I am writing this. They came for me when they could look into my eyes and see they had lost me. When I rejected them and chose chaos instead, they were still there to be found once I wandered back out into reality again. They are here to talk to me now, as I have struggled with a decade of illness and chronic pain.

And my wife, Mendy, has been a rock for me as I've struggled to be any good for her. I'm trying. Writing this book has been part of trying. Some of my medical struggle has brought my past and my future into a state of clarity that can only be achieved through pain. And this story has poured out of me like an open floodgate. It has brought Mendy and I together through the physical struggle, instead of allowing me to push us apart like I might otherwise try to do. It's past time for the gods of chaos to lose a few battles. We'll get to her part of the story soon.

So, I graduated high school and had to decide if I was going to be an actor, a broker, an attorney, a minister, an M.P., a bouncer, a cop, a businessman, a gambler, or a criminal. Some of those might mix and match. Some of them required college, so college was next.

CHAPTER 4:
BELIEVING IN SOMETHING AFTER

IN THE OLD COUNTRY church on Straight Creek, when I was little, I played on the floor under the pews while a Baptist preacher did his best to bring God into the hearts of the people sitting above me. I played with a friend under there. We'd get redirected and scolded, to get us to sit still. On occasion, someone who wasn't a part of my family gave us both graham crackers to get us to sit still. It didn't happen every Sunday, and not nearly as often as I wanted, but it worked. I thought that was the best thing ever. As a small child, I couldn't imagine ever getting anything better out of church. There are some Sundays I start to wonder if that kid I used to be under the pew didn't already have the whole scene figured out.

My grandpa eventually became a country preacher. The last 20 years of his life he lived out in an old "temporary" housing building that had been built by the logging companies back when they were clearing the area. They left, the building stayed, and my grandparents counted out their days there. Even up in the informal Kentucky hills, in his final days, he never left the house without wearing a hat and a coat. It just wasn't proper.

He didn't have any hobbies and they didn't watch TV, so he read his Bible. He wore out one copy from constant use and as I write this, I have the replacement Bible that took over after the first one gave up the ghost between my grandpa's faithful fingers. He knew his Bible and quoted it as often as it applied, which was in nearly every conceivable situation by his calculation.

In all our travels, my family members weren't regular attenders anywhere for a long while. We weren't even Easter and Christmas Christians. We were maybe every fourth Easter Christians at best.

I didn't really go back to church again until the summer I was visiting my grandparents in Kentucky, in 1988. I was sixteen years old and my friends said I'd like Vacation Bible School because there was fun, food, and games. They weren't lying. All that was there. The sermon was short and the minister gave an altar call for anyone who wasn't saved. I felt led and I walked down to accept Jesus.

I believe to this day my decision was real and authentic. I believe my conversion was sincere and uncalculated. I struggle with my personality, and my mindset as a businessman, seeing many of my actions as calculating. Every decision we make is calculated to a degree. Being kind to someone when our instinct is to be selfish is a calculation. When we work to improve or save our relationships, even with pure motives, it is a calculation. I struggle with my innate desire to be honest, transparent, and authentic, especially with the people I love, and my tendency to calculate the odds and act accordingly. My acceptance of faith in that moment, though, was a complete surrender. The closest I have come to that moment, since then, is in my current effort to begin to be the best I can be for my family.

So, I went back to Georgia after the summer of my salvation and returned to living like a heathen. I spoke of God often with my circles of friends. They gave me the nickname "Padre," And then, I would go raise hell with them at every opportunity.

I followed a girlfriend to Glover Baptist Church, where I joined on October 14, 1990. I found that written inside the cover of a Bible. My parents indirectly followed me there. They still attend the church that Glover Baptist eventually merged with.

Looking back, I'm surprised at how many times I made a point of drinking in a church parking lot. I drank before or after church activities, sometimes. I don't really know why. Most of those times, I wasn't drinking to get drunk. Maybe it was an act of defiance. I'm not sure if that was against those who spoke for God, or if I was keeping it clear to God himself, who called the shots outside the doors. Sometimes I'm here for the miracles and sometimes I'm jonesing for a graham cracker.

I've read my Bible from cover to cover more than once. In between, I've started and stopped it a few times. Through all my low points, I've never reached a place where I didn't believe that God was real. Whether he is "the God of my Fathers" as portrayed from page and pulpit, I'm not certain. What God looks like, and how I perceive him, have changed for me over time. But I never lost my belief that there is something after. I believe there is a real transition from where we are now, to where we will be after, but I don't know exactly what that is from where I stand now. That idea has been instrumental for me in transitioning from the low points where I found myself in life, to where I needed to go with lifestyle, business, and relationships. Legacy is all about believing in something after. Success is about believing there is something after failure, too.

After high school, I went to Gordon College in the fall, on a theater scholarship and lasted one quarter. I bounced around for a while. I was an extra in the Sandra Bullock movie Love Potion #9. I landed in Florida and made a go at standup comedy. Almost had a hosting job on a TV show, but let that go.

While I was in Florida, I rented a house and invited friends from school to come crash and party. I met Davie Smith, visiting from Northern Ireland on a visa. He claimed to have ties to the IRA (Irish Republican Army) back in Belfast, famous for terror attacks through the mid-to-late twentieth century there.

He was the kind of chaos I gravitated toward. Davie's visa was expiring, but he wanted to see America, even though he had no way to get around. Well, he had Brent Brock. We were off.

He could very well be the only person I might dare to say could be stone-cold crazier than Carl Brock was. We set out for Colorado in my 1993 grey Ford Escort. I had recently purchased it new—my first new car. Lots of fun and lots of interesting situations. We teamed up, hustling pool halls from Florida to Colorado. Turns out Colorado took that stuff seriously. The Rockies were still beautiful the way I remembered them.

We stole from gas stations. I rode in my first hot-wired car that Davie acquired.

While passing through Kentucky on the way, I almost shot a man for talking bad about my dad. We were on property we weren't supposed to be on, with some old friends. This guy and a friend of his came out of the woods on four-wheelers and hung out at the fire with us before he started jawing off at me about Carl Brock.

It hadn't been long since I wished the man dead, myself, during his final hospital stay. But I was willing to contemplate taking a life from a guy saying out loud, what I deep down believed to be true. As a general rule, don't talk about crazy people's family. They will hate you with as much passion as they hate each other.

I didn't want to kill the guy, but I came very close. I had the gun in my pocket and was ready to take him out. My finger was on the trigger. We were three feet apart and I pointed it at his face. First time I literally had someone else's life in my hands, and I was steaming. My hand was still, but my knees were watery.

Davie was so mad at me for not shooting that guy. He actually tried to take the gun from me to do it himself.

I'm not proud to say that more than one person has had a weapon pointed at them because of me. I've had more than a few pointed at me, too. First time I ended up handcuffed and put in the back of a car was after I was at Gordon College, but it wouldn't be the

Location: B8

VOM.3OC

Title:	How to Make No Friends Everywhere
Cond:	Good
User:	vo_list
Station:	DESKTOP-95EUL5F
Date:	2020-07-27 17.44:03 (UTC)
Account:	Veteran-Outsource
Orig Loc:	B8
mSKU:	VOM.3OC
Seq#:	192
QuickPick	J2T
unit_id:	664990
width:	0.35 in

delist unit# 664990

XXXXX

VOM3OC

last. If there was a degree in bar fights, I'd at least have a Bachelor's.

Back in Florida, Davie stole a cop car in Daytona Beach and drove it into the ocean. He ended up getting deported back to Northern Ireland. I spoke to him only once more, years later, after he got back to Belfast. To this day, I'm not 100% certain Davie Smith was actually his real name.

I moved back to Georgia. I was confused about what to do. I considered the army, and they recruited me, but I didn't go.

In 1994, I decided to go back to school. Fall classes were already starting everywhere and registration was already long ago closed, but my old youth minister from Glover Baptist, Mark Wood, helped me look for something.

I considered seminary and he took me to look at a campus in the Atlanta area. I had felt what I interpreted as a call into ministry for many years, despite all my Davie Smith-style side trips through my life. One deciding factor for me, beyond any questions of fitness for the job, was the money. With my mentality toward money, I would have become a crooked TV evangelist before I ever became a country preacher like my grandfather.

We went up to Truett-McConnell College, a little Baptist college deep in the hills of North East Georgia. That location description is literally in the school song. It was a two-year school, which had a low bar for admission. Students who flunked out of other colleges went there to get their GPAs back up, so they could get back in where they really wanted to go. Classes had essentially started, but Mark talked to them for me and introduced me, and I got in.

It is the kind of place where I almost got into a fistfight whenever I questioned whether the Word of God was infallible, or if the King James Version of the Bible wasn't the only acceptable one like my grandpa claimed, or if every word wasn't literal. It is also a place where you can find trouble with the crew trying to get their GPA up, deep in the hills of North East Georgia.

The school was about to switch over from quarters to semesters. I had enough credits to get an associates degree, but I didn't want a degree from there. So, I left with my pile of credits.

I went to Berry College in Rome, Georgia, in another corner of North Georgia, on a scholarship. I didn't stay long and ended up crashing at a house in Dahlonega, Georgia for a while, among other places. There were bonfires, girls, drinking, and more of my kind of trouble.

I came back to Rome, but settled at Shorter College this time. I enrolled late there, as well, but also with an academic scholarship.

I dated a couple girls right away when I got there. I was a pseudo member of a pseudo fraternity called KO. None of the fraternities or sororities at this Baptist school were matched up to any national Greek organizations. I was a pseudo member, in that I showed up if there was going to be partying or drinking or fighting.

My friend in KO was dating the roommate of the girl who would become my first wife. We were at the Applebee's one night and my friend saw his girl come in. My back was to the door and when I turned, I saw Stacie. At that moment, I thought, can I get this girl to like me? One of the other guys commented that she was way out of my league. He was right, but that just spurred me on.

That night we all sat together and closed out the Applebee's. I just got into her car. She asked me what I thought I was doing. I told her she was taking me back to campus. She said she wasn't. She stood there a while, going back and forth with me, but eventually, she drove me back to campus. I feel like I got into her head, like a snippet of song lyric that gets caught there and you just can't get it out.

She was still dating her first boyfriend from back home, a big burly guy named Matt, who was still in high school. I was late getting to the last half of my college years and still having to catch up on classes, so I was about six years older than her.

We started dating before she broke up with Matt. For a time, she went back and forth between us. I was there when she broke up with him. She called him to come up from where they lived in Cobb County. I was there for moral support, so I was sitting in the lobby when the guy came in. He passed me without realizing who I was. I couldn't hear them talking, but the conversation went on for a few minutes. Then, he left, and that was it. She had set her destiny and she was stuck with me. Like every relationship before, we fought, broke up for periods of time, and got back together.

I moved off campus, behind a mental institution, which was ironically appropriate. In my defense, I wouldn't actually be in one until years later. I would ultimately graduate in 1998, but Stacie would drop out and end up living with me while I was finishing school. Dropping out and being with me were two details that did not set well with her father.

I worked as a food runner at Checkers Nightclub, in Rome. They were shorthanded on security one night and picked me to fill in, mostly because they had no other option. The club would later be bought by Governors, which was a country bar that had been located in another part of Rome, Georgia. They fired everyone, top-to-bottom, in the club except for two people and I was one they kept on.

As I was attempting to break up a fight between a couple guys one night, I managed to get hit with a stool by one of them. I lost it with this dude, who was much, much bigger than me. I had to take him to the ground. We had a cactus in the corner that was for decorative purposes. I didn't have to accidentally run his face into and across the cactus several times, but I did.

I heard a real rough voice from someone who had to have smoked four packs a day say, "Damn it, Brock. What are you doing?"

I looked up to see Officer Kelly Flowers standing over me, with this dude pinned under me, his face gushing with blood. I explained how he started the fight and I had to defend myself. You know, with a cactus, like any sane person would.

Flowers and I had spent a couple evenings together on a ride-along with the Rome Police Department, as part of one of my courses in school. I had been to his home when we were supposed to be on patrol. Flowers arrested the guy with his face in the cactus and not me.

I was personally named in a lawsuit from a person who had been in the club. The judge threw out the case on a technicality.

A friend of mine owned a Victorian house in the ghetto of Rome. It was a rough neighborhood, but it would feel like home to me. He did some renovations and divided it in two to make a duplex and rented out the other side. Eventually, I owned it and rented the other side for enough to cover the mortgage.

One of the teachers on campus got me a job at a liquor store, with a man who the teacher had worked for back when he was a student at Shorter. The owner of the store came from old money in Rome. I learned a little about stock trading and how options worked from him, which would indirectly lead to me being a broker later. He explained his system to me. As he reflected on his life, he decided he wanted to retire. He ran off to the Keys for a while and I ran the store for him, along with some other idiot. He came back once a month or so to check in. Eventually, I hired my entire posse to work there with me.

One of the sororities at Shorter, the one that had little sisters for our fraternity, held an annual event at a fancy restaurant set up on a hill in Rome, Georgia. They rented out the restaurant for their Yellow Ribbon Daisy Day, or whatever it was.

Some series of events led to a drunken fight and me breaking beer bottles off the skulls of the guys I was fighting. I made my getaway down the fire escape because I knew the guy who was guarding that door. The cops caught up with me about two streets over. I was running through a neighborhood in the rain. I ran into the chain link fence and some high grass. As I lay on the ground in the rain, in the mud, a cop car slowed down looking for me and a spotlight went over my head. It's hard to come up with a good way to explain how much I felt hunted in that moment.

The rain started coming down really hard. I didn't want to get caught out in the open, though. I passed out in the grass for a period of time. I woke up again and belly-crawled in the mud to the nearest payphone I could find. I called someone to come pick me up.

I heard that the cops had interviewed a number of people at the restaurant and were looking for me. This was near graduation and I was afraid I wouldn't be able to graduate. I went to West Georgia College to stay with my old roommate from Truett. He was playing baseball there. My plan was to lay low for a couple of days, and then go back to Rome for graduation. Then, I'd get the hell out of there. Before I left West Georgia, I ended up starting a near-riot at a baseball game by getting another fight going.

I came to find out one or two of my friends in the crowd at the restaurant confused the situation by throwing another guy's name into the mix. The cops never came looking for me, that I'm aware of. Another opportunity where I could have tanked my college career, only days away from graduating.

I could fill the whole book with stories of bad decisions before, during, and after my college years. I think the ones I shared get the point across, if you extrapolate them out to represent many more examples. At a certain point, telling every wild story you got goes from being confessional, to just bragging. That's not my goal. I'll go into more detail about the impact of alcohol and such on my personality in another chapter.

I was content to stay in Rome after graduation, but Stacie was homesick, so we moved back to the county her family, literally, founded. Her parents were founding members of Burnt Hickory Baptist Church. Her dad was a multimillionaire. Her ancestors divided up the land that would be Cobb County, Georgia, between them.

We rented out both sides of the Victorian and moved into a house on Burnt Hickory Road. We could see her parents' house and the church we would be married inside in 2000. To her parents' distress, we moved into that house in Cobb together in 1998, two years before getting married.

My future father-in-law did not like me, but wanted to keep me close so he could watch me and his daughter. He back-boarded me on the deal with the house and worked out the details with Stacie. I wrote him checks each month for the rent. After a while, his secretary called me to ask what he was supposed to do with the checks I wrote. I told her they were for rent. She asked if they would clear, because he was going to put them all through. I said that was the plan when I paid the rent. I didn't understand why they hadn't been deposited all along. So, he did put them all through at once and to his surprise, they all cleared. He saw me as a broke college kid, which wasn't far from the truth, but I always worked to save money.

Out of college, I struggled to find work. I worked hourly and odd jobs. I got rejected from several. I worked as a broker for a while and then would

BRENT BROCK & JAY WILBURN

eventually work for Stacie's dad. He would grow to
like me, then hate me, and then feel I had screwed
him over. Though he showed his colors in the end.

Before I became a broker, I got turned down for a
job as a used car salesman. That hit hard. I thought,
I'm not even good enough for this crowd? There are a
couple truths about my life that I am sure of. One is
that when I didn't go to seminary, God dodged a
bullet. The other is when I got turned down to sell
used cars, I dodged a bullet, but that dealership
missed out on a real opportunity.

In the phase of liking me, her dad would call at
8:00 at night and say he wanted to go to Seattle. So,
the whole family would go the next day. It turned out
he was covering for a secret life I would grow to
suspect. I caught a look at his books and realized what
he was trying to do.

In 2003, I went to my first wife and asked her,
hypothetically, if there was something I knew about
her father that would shatter the way she saw him
forever, would she want me to tell her. She said, no. I
had a similar conversation with my mother-in-law.
She ran me out of the house. It would all come out
later, and I'll save that story for later in the book.

I was toxic to be around, for Stacie or for anyone,
especially when I was drinking. We separated the first
time in 2004, from February to August of that year. I
went everywhere during that time. Trying to find
myself, but always stuck with me.

We got back together because of my sister Laura's
40th birthday party, down at her house in Florida.
Stacie was, and still is, close friends with Laura. I
think it is great because our kids, who live mostly with

their mother, still get to see the rest of their family. To this day, we all still have Thanksgiving together there in Florida. I know it is weird for my wife, Mendy. Being married to me makes everything weird, I'm afraid.

I saw Stacie at the party. We didn't talk much. It was tense and surreal. Not the sort of thing you'd expect to spur a reconciliation. Everyone was drinking, but ironically, I was not. Someone opened a cooler and handed me a beer, but I refused it. Stacie saw that.

Later that night, she called me from my sister's house where she was staying. She was very drunk. She talked about having dinner or lunch some time. I wasn't sure she would still want to once she was sober, but she did. We visited one another a few times and decided to get back together.

I stayed dry and sober from 2004 until 2014, after we were divorced. There was no drinking. There was no cheating. Everything that caused us to fall apart had no excuses other than I was who I was.

My health issues began in 2007, as described back in the introduction. Our twins were born in 2008.

My commitment to businesses I bought and took over added to the strain on our marriage. I committed finances without fully getting her permission. I hate getting permission. I'll go into the details of my rise in business in another chapter, but the finances put a toll on her, our marriage, and me. I didn't fully realize how much personal identity and security and mental wellbeing I connected to money. I spent most of my life poor, and my obsession with saving had dug deep. Before I ever missed a bill, I was nearly suicidal over financial strain. Our marriage bond was too thin, already, to bear any additional strain.

That brought things to a head in 2013. We hadn't discussed divorce, outside my angry outbursts on occasions. We just drifted forward through our lives with our family. We survived each other from year to year, instead of really living together anymore.

I had to go to Charter Peachford for five days. I had suicidal ideations and was at the end of my mental capacity. After I got out, I wasn't able to leave my bedroom for three weeks. I read everything I could on anxiety. I thought I was sentenced to this state forever. And I had very few breaks from the intensity of my mental struggles at that time.

I wanted to be around Stacie all the time, and I managed my businesses by phone as I tried to pull myself together.

I went out with a friend for coffee, but I couldn't handle it for long. I had to get back to my bedroom. I had to get back into that cell I hated.

When she went shopping, I had to go with her, because I couldn't be alone. I wanted to hold her hand. As she was in the changing room, trying on clothes, I pulled up a chair as close as I could get.

It wasn't about love, though. It was desperation. It was mental health stuff. I was clinging for selfish reasons. At best, it was too little too late. At worst, it was me still being selfish. I had dragged her along for over a decade, and she had already left me in her mind and heart.

The old ladies who worked at the store, talking to me while my wife changed, made me feel better. It made me feel like I was there. They see me. I must be here. I must exist. There must be something after this moment of deep trouble, because people can still see me.

I imagine Stacie had to question everything she had done since meeting me. She had to ask herself why she ever gave up big, burly, loving Matt from high school for the walking wildfire that was Brent Brock.

I ignored her for years upon years, but now she had my relentless attention. My active pursuit to her active retreat. And I was only pursuing because I didn't want to be alone. Any voice would do. It made me feel all the more alone.

I came through it, though. Business got better. I got better.

We separated for the final time in 2014.

We still hadn't discussed divorce. A friend of mine was going through the collapse of his own marriage. With my marriage coming apart, I poured myself into helping him, instead. I'd stay late helping him figure out what to do next. It would get late and I would step outside. He would follow and we'd talk another hour. I'd go to the car and he'd sit in the car with me. We'd talk another hour.

I'd return home to my own neglected wife then, too.

One day, my friend's marriage came up as I was sharing about our discussions. Stacie came out and said to me, "Why don't you just move in with him?"

That was how we did it. After all my years of trying to push her away, the same way I pushed everyone and everything away from me, that's how we discussed divorce for the first real time. I did move in with him and we divorced that same year.

I did not react well, but that will fit better in another chapter, too.

Stacie is a good mother. We have worked hard to co-parent through everything.

I was divorced for about a year-and-a-half before I started dating Mendy. We were engaged and married in under a year. She has had to deal with Brent Brock, too. I have recently started working on Brent to make myself more like the husband she really deserves.

There are many differences between Mendy and other people in my life. The difference between a marriage that lasts, and all the ones that don't, comes down to people refusing to give up. I still played my game of trying to push the people who loved me away. Mendy is not one who leaves. Anything short of me forcing her out, she intends to stay and make things right. She is better than me. She deserves her own chapter to explore how great she really is.

The fact that she won't give up on me is the perfect foundation for making things right. It is all the potential needed for us to be good together—good as a family.

This book is as much about that, as it is about anything.

When you finally decide to fight for someone who will never give up on you, anything can happen. She is saving me as I struggle with my past and with my health. I'm trying to become the kind of man that can save her, too. The kind of husband that honors all she has sacrificed to be here for me and the kids.

I could not see what was after the anxiety when I got out of Charter Peachford. I could not see what was beyond divorce after Stacie left. Mendy was the proof that something great can come after every hard time I have been through.

She is the answer to many of my questions.

Is this all worth it?

Can life get better?

And what are we doing this for?

I intend to work until I'm the answer for her, too. I want to become the reward for all the work she has put into supporting me.

There is more to tell about how I got here, though.

CHAPTER 5:

CUT OFF

I FELT LIKE I was on fire, and everywhere I went I was burning. Everything I threw on that fire to put it out, just made it worse. Unfortunately, I tended to pour alcohol on the flames, too.

The saying goes, every time I drank, I didn't get into trouble, but every time I got into trouble, I'd been drinking. That may not be entirely true because I can stir up plenty of trouble stone cold sober, but it is close enough to the truth to serve as a warning and a wake-up call for me.

To my mother's credit, she tried to intervene with me early. She took me to an off-site counseling program when I was in seventh grade. They were collecting research and data on alcoholic fathers and their sons. Thinking back, I believe their study may have been descriptive instead of prescriptive, so it didn't go much into the preventative measures my mother may have hoped for. The program was called Missing Link. Can you think of a dumber name for a program about kids and alcohol? I wasn't drinking at the time.

Other than sipping from the beers from relatives

ever since I was little, my first attempt to get alcohol and to get drunk all on my own was not long after "Missing Link," in those North Springs apartments across from the high school. My buddies and I gathered what amounted to a few beers to split between us from all our houses.

One of our friends saw maintenance leave a vacant apartment open. We lied to our parents in an elaborate scheme about whose house we were staying at for a sleepover.

The beer was piss-warm and tasted awful. None of us got drunk.

I decided to set up sentries to keep us from getting caught. I created the schedule. Each man was supposed wake up the next guy on the schedule, and stay up with him a few minutes to be sure he was awake. I took the first shift. I woke up the next guy, but he fell asleep after I left him. We woke up with daylight coming in on our few crushed beer cans. I was so mad. We got out without getting caught, though.

Once I started drinking, from then on, my goal was always to get drunk. I started figuring out where all the parties were. We stood outside the liquor store and made deals with the guys going in and out. We paid for their cigarettes, or paid extra to get them to buy for us. My Uncle Kevin, the one who supplied me with joints to sell in high school, could get us kegs, too, when we wanted them.

I did use harder drugs while I was at North Springs. My friends decided they wanted to be in a glam metal hair band. I was going to be their manager. That went nowhere. We ended up with cocaine at one of the clubs we attended. As soon as it hit my brain and nervous system, I thought, I have to get more. I started planning to get more. I had to get more. We planned to meet up with the guy again the next week, but I didn't go.

Over the next several years, I used it rarely. It would be for a week or two at a time, and then I'd just stop for months or years. I don't have a clear explanation of why. Something gave me an awareness that I wanted it too much.

Alcohol told me, "Hey, I'm your buddy. We're old friends. Look at all the good times and great stories we have. I'm here for you whenever you need me. We're cool."

Cocaine said, "I own you."

Alcohol probably did own me, in reality, but it was polite enough not to come right out and say it like that. If I had taken to other drugs like I took to alcohol, I'd probably be dead right now.

Once, I was in a motel with cocaine again, and a woman to share it with. A couple of my oldest friends came to get me. They convinced me to go outside with them and to the corner away from the room. They wanted me to leave with them, but I refused. They came close to taking me by force, but I think they arrived at the conclusion that it would not go well for them.

I got back in the room and one of them got what was left of my eight-balls. He held them up and said, "I'm going to flush it."

I said, "Go ahead."

"I'm going to do it."

"I don't give a fuck. Go ahead."

I think he expected a fight from me. He took it to the bathroom and looked at me again.

"I don't care. Do it."

He flushed the rest of my drugs and, despite having been up all night drinking and doing drugs, I honestly didn't care.

They left me there in that hotel. I didn't care about them taking the drugs away, but I wasn't going with them.

One of my friends, the one I went to stay with when I divorced my first wife, said to me later that he looked into my eyes that day and realized he had lost me. He and I are close and in contact now, but it would be a while after that morning in the motel before we reconnected.

The last time I did cocaine, I remember my clearest thought being that this wasn't as good as when I was young. I got rid of what I had left and that was it.

I can't explain my personality or psyche when it comes to other drugs versus alcohol. There is just zero risk of other drugs being a problem for me in the future, but alcohol is the old friend I just can't trust myself with. It's around to tell me we are old buddies and to remind me of all the "fun" we have together. But I have to keep my guard up around it. It's tough, because we go way back. It was good friends with my father, too, and we have history.

I didn't start smoking cigarettes until I was 24. I struggled with them for about ten years and then quit for good. I didn't follow a clear pattern with any addiction, other than alcohol.

I went to a lot of parties through high school and

college. There were always more guys than girls, so I felt the challenge to stand out and win the attention of the girls. This made me oddly aggressive with the other guys I was drinking with, even if they were the kind who had no chance with the girls.

My freshman year of high school I was at a party with one of my close friends. He went to the bathroom and I pissed in his drink with everyone watching. I wanted them to see. He came back and started drinking it. No one told him, no one challenged me about it, and the snickering started. When he realized it, I confessed. It got tense. He made a joke about it and finished off his drink, saving the mood.

No one would have said anything to me. If challenged while I was drunk, I would have fought anyone. There were bigger guys there, but they wanted no part of my trouble. If I started something, people would just let it go because there would be no reigning it in. I'm not always pleasant when I am sober, but what little bit lies over the anger, hate, and revenge in my life is stripped away when I am drunk. Then, it is unchained and undirected anger. It was vengeance for being born. It was hate of having to be me, because my life was always on fire.

It took me years to become aware I was having blackouts when I drank. I was almost immediately remorseful after I opened my eyes. I worked to piece together the details, to see what damage to my life needed to be fixed this time. Friends would tell me the familiar story that I wanted to fight everyone. I was a danger to myself and everyone around me.

The biggest problem may have been my ability to talk myself out of situations, even when I was out of my skull. I'd talk things over with police. I'd talk myself out of trouble while hungover. I'd negotiate my way down to small trouble, instead of life-ending trouble. Maybe bigger trouble would have stopped me sooner, but I doubt it. My ability to reason my way out of the consequences of my destruction may have been superhuman, though.

Before I was out of high school, I figured out I had a drinking problem. I still liked it, though, and felt at home in that chaos still. The only drinking problem that concerned me was that I had two hands, but only one mouth. I surrounded myself with people like me, who drank hard, partied hard, and fought hard. Otherwise, we didn't hang out. Not for long, anyway.

In eleventh grade, I had a friend on the wrestling team I drank with. Later, we would work together with a coffee company, but that story will be better for another chapter. We smoked weed together once. Like other drugs, I just had no interest in it. It didn't hook me. We shot pool together a lot.

I hung out with him and his sister. I had a sense that his sister was on a bad path. If she was bad enough that I noticed, it had to be bad, but I didn't get that he was having real trouble, too.

One night we had stopped to pump gas and were making plans to get together again. I had no idea that I wouldn't see them again for years after that night.

I hadn't heard from them for a while and started calling. His mother finally told me that they had checked both kids into Charter Peachford for treatment. She made a point to tell me it was at great expense. They would end up retiring late because of the cost of putting both their kids into rehab at the same time.

She also told me that they were not going to be able to hang out with old friends who got them into trouble and were bad influences. That included me. I didn't even argue. I just said, okay.

I did run into him at a church we were both at, years later. He was freshly indoctrinated into AA, NA, and every "A" out there. He asked me to come along with him to a meeting, for support. Looking back, it is clear that he wanted to get me into a meeting. He was quite comfortable going without me, I realize now.

We went to a café afterward. People welcomed me in because they thought I was there. In my mind, I was just visiting with a friend. I was taken aback by the level of openness I hadn't experienced anywhere else. People welcomed me in, but I didn't share. One guy there was a broker. Another was a doctor who had been self-prescribing.

It would be a while before "I was there."

When I worked at the liquor store in Rome, Georgia, I was allowed to drink while I was at work. In fact, the owner encouraged that I sample the wines, so I could speak about them intelligently to our discerning customers with discerning pallets. The store sold more wine than any other liquor store between Rome and Chattanooga, according to our distributors. My business dealings with the store were above reproach.

Only one time in my life, unrelated to that store, did I ever drink a couple bottles of wine to get drunk. I'm apparently a very discerning and picky addict, but a very liberal fighter and brawler. And I never met a bar fight I didn't love.

In 2004, after a long and troublesome binge during my separation from my first wife, I ended up on an airplane straight to Florida and my sister's house, without showering. I apologized to everyone I sat by on that journey because of how bad I smelled. She had done the research and got me into a treatment center. My time there was hard. There was a lot to dig through. There was a lot of damage to spread out in the light and sort through.

Eventually, I'd spend a decade or more in recovery rooms and meetings.

I was clean for a few months, had a few more falls, and then I was clean from 2004 through 2014. My first marriage still came apart during that time. My life almost did, too. Dry drunk syndrome is the term for a guy that has dried out from the craving for alcohol, but still suffers from the underlying psychological issues connected with their addiction. I was the model of the dry drunk, especially in my relationships.

When I fell off the wagon again in 2014, I didn't feel like it was because of the divorce at the time. I went a long while without drinking after the divorce. I was in the "bachelor pad" with the friend my first wife had sent me off to live with. Another guy whose marriage fell apart joined us. They went out drinking and I drove. For a long time, we would shutdown the bar and I just sat there drinking my water or tea.

If you sit in a barbershop long enough, you'll get a haircut. That's how the warning goes. We weren't even in a bar. We were just at a restaurant having dinner, just my friend and me. My friend ordered a beer and I did, too.

The waitress walked away, and my friend asked, "Are you sure you want to do that?"

I thought about it briefly. "Yeah, I am."

"Okay."

And that was it. It was as simple and as quiet as that.

My shenanigans after that were contained, to a degree. The wheels came off, but out from under the eyes of most people in my life. I did my damage, but I did it in a vacuum.

The binge in 2014 ended quickly. I was back in jail after another bar fight—last time I was arrested, for what it is worth. I was starting to make money, hired an attorney, and let a professional talk me out of trouble this time. I was sentenced to a couple classes instead of anything more serious.

My ex-wife didn't know. As we planned life after marriage, she said to me, "If I ever find out you are drinking, that's it."

After a while, my behavior improved in her eyes and our relationship as parents improved where our relationship as husband and wife never could.

Mendy had to deal with my drinking a little before and after we were married. I remember the last time I got drunk, but don't even remember the last time I had a sip.

Mendy and I were in Charleston. We were on the rooftop bar of our hotel. We'd had some drinks during the day, and more that evening, and I lost track. My drinking got away from me, like so many times before.

I was running my mouth and having "fun," but hadn't gotten into any trouble with anyone yet. There were a couple different couples we were having a good time with.

I went to order a few more doubles. I got a tray of them for the table, but we were one short. I pointed it out. The man and woman behind the bar talked to each other and then the guy stepped up. He said, "You're cut off."

I demanded to know why, but he wouldn't tell me. From my perspective, he was just bowing up on me for no reason. We exchanged words. I threatened him and he believed me.

I was pissed. The other guy at our table egged me on by saying he didn't understand why I was cut off, either.

I went back to continue my argument. It escalated until I was threatening every guy on that deck. Mendy tried to usher me out.

Another guy, much bigger than me, stepped up and told me I needed to knock it off.

I pointed my finger at him and said, "This is between me and him. It's my and his problem. Do you want it to be your problem, too?"

The guy smiled and said, "You know? Put that way, no, I don't."

Mendy got me back to my room and I pulled out my gun as I screamed about how people were treating me. I had no intention of using it, so I shouldn't have taken it out. I gave her the bullets and magazine to reassure her that I wasn't going to do anything. I'm sure she didn't sleep at all that night.

The guy we were sitting with came to our door to be

sure everything was okay. Mendy talked to him through the partially open door. He was still talking about getting our number to stay in touch. He then saw me, and saw the gun laying out in the open. He turned around and bolted out of our lives without another word.

I later went downstairs to talk to security and deescalated the situation, as I am skilled at doing even when I'm at my worst.

The next morning the hotel manager called me while I was still hungover. The bartender had called out of work and wouldn't come back until we left. We still had one more night and I talked the manager into not kicking us out.

I kept asking him what I had done before I was cut off. He was reluctant to tell me, but eventually said, "Your wife asked us to."

I was floored. I felt betrayed at the time, but now I see the betrayal was to her.

There are more stories with the same point and moral as this one, when it comes to my drinking. This was the last one, though, and it makes the point well enough. I can't remember the last time I had a sip. I'm well aware of the dangers of "sitting in the barbershop." And the message has been driven home for me again.

I don't like who I am when I'm drunk. Sometimes I don't like who I am when I'm sober, but I can at least work on improving the sober version of me. I don't like picking up the pieces of my life afterward, either.

I don't desire the high, nor the consequences, anymore. I tried to convince myself that I like the taste of a smooth bourbon like civilized drinking adults do, but I really don't.

HOW TO MAKE NO FRIENDS EVERYWHERE

The question I had to ask myself was whether there is anything I love about a cold beer at the end of a day, an appreciation for a glass of wine, or the "fun" I have while drinking, that is worth more than my wife and my kids.

If we are honest with ourselves, that answer is easy, but the work to achieve it and live it is hard.

My best stories came from drinking, but none of the things I'm proud of did. I'm not proud of everything I have done while sober, but everything I've achieved that I am proud of never started with drinking.

Only the sober version of me stands a chance with my wife and kids. Only that guy has any potential to leave a legacy instead of a shadow.

CHAPTER 6:

NEVER BROKE, NEVER BROKEN

SINCE THE DAY I started my paper route as a kid back in Louisiana, I have never been completely broke. I've made bad choices with money. I've gotten into pinches. I've taken myself to my personal breaking point. But I have compulsively saved since the day I started making my own money.

After my twins were born, I was so worried over money I made my mom wash out, hang, and dry paper towels to reuse. That lasted about a month, I think. Now I use three or four at a time. No offense to the trees, but there are better ways to save money than reusing paper towels for the time, energy, and capital.

Maybe growing up poor had something to do with it. I could embody the hustle I saw in some good role models behind me. I know that one of my sincerest desires from a young age was to be able to take care of my parents, Mom and Junior, when they got old. I started keeping up with my money back then, but I'm only just now reaching that goal.

Junior, my stepdad, is as hard a worker as I know, and I turn to him even now for his labor skills. He blows through money, though, and he knows it. Any time I bring him money, he says, "Give it to your mother. You know how I am."

He's not the only one in my family like that. I love my parents dearly.

I started investing money when I was seventeen years old. The last few years have shown the returns on those early investments and saving habits.

Part of my problem when I was younger was that I never stayed in one place long enough to really capitalize on my efforts—not fully. I kept myself in a mental state of being broke and constantly worked to stay above that station, even in my worst circumstances. I paid for everything in my life because my parents were hardly ever in a position to do so.

A relative recently asked me what it was like to be rich. This is a good example of how that term is subjective, based on the financial status of the observer. I was helping him with something, and my picture came up on his computer screen. I kept trying to clear it because I thought I had somehow pulled up one of my accounts. Then, I realized his background/ screensaver on his computer was my picture. I held that kind of position in his life.

He hadn't intended for me to see it. But I looked back and realized, throughout our lives he had been reaching out to me for my attention. He was one of the few people in my life who never asked me for anything. That weighed heavily on me.

So much of my life felt like a disaster to me, in so many areas, I sometimes forgot how big my successes in business looked to people who went through those crazy times with me and were still struggling themselves.

Everything I learned in business seemed to come from making mistakes before I learned to do it the right way, or a better way. I did learn, though. As time went on, successes led to more success and I was able to improve upon things that worked, instead of always learning from mistakes. Failure is a great teacher, if you are willing to learn from it and move on, though.

Between the time I was at Gordon College and Truett-McConnell, I started working for a coffee company, in the early 90s. I was in bartending school and got recruited from there through one of the teachers. This was before it was possible to get cappuccinos anywhere, anytime you wanted. They had a few self-contained carts and had worked out a deal with the World Congress Center in Atlanta to have them out during major events. By the time I left, they had 18 carts and were going on 22. It wasn't uncommon for us to have over a hundred thousand dollars after an event at the Congress Center. I also had several promises made to me from them that weren't kept. It wouldn't be the first, or last, time that happened.

It was an all-cash business, but credit cards weren't as ubiquitous for quick purchases like they are today. They opened a place at one of the Atlanta malls and I managed that, too. One night, I wasn't able to get a deposit in and had to bring home two big zipped bank bags full of money. I cataloged everything and counted it out to be sure they saw everything was there when it did get deposited. As I was counting it out, my sister Lisa's second husband, a drug addict, came in and stared at the money for a long time. He had been stealing from my personal money at that point. He just marveled at how that might be more money than he could earn in months, if ever. He didn't get any of the company money that night, or ever.

They eventually got the Georgia Dome contract, which I felt was a mistake. There weren't enough events there, and not enough where coffee was going to compete with beer at the time. We did very well when the Amway convention came through once a year. But they lost out on that deal.

We were looking at expanding into Florida before I left. We discussed the expansion of Starbucks. By this point, Starbucks had only come as far east as O'Hare, in Chicago. It was the conclusion of my bosses that Starbucks would never come to the South because it was too hot for coffee to be profitable on their scale. I disagreed, and we all see how that worked out.

They did not keep their promises, and they were not generous with the profits I brought to them. It was not in my best interests to continue working for them as I had.

I worked for a struggling local newspaper while I was going to Truett-McConnell. The guy running it was in his twenties and he was in over his head. I worked into the night getting articles and other copy set up for printings. This paper was connected to a few others that all got printed out of Gainesville, Georgia. The paper insisted I drive to Gainesville and help with the printing. I was working until nine or ten o'clock at night, in the office by myself, before these requests came in.

I didn't understand Mac at all. I had never seen a Mac computer before. I had to recruit one of the smart kids from school to come show me how to navigate it.

I made more money on my paper route back in Louisiana. The camera the County News issued me looked like it came from the thrift barn back in Kentucky.

In Rome, Georgia, at Shorter College, I worked at the liquor store until the idiot, who worked with me as the owner semi-retired, fired me. The guy was a friend of the owner. It didn't take the owner long to figure out his friend was a raging alcoholic, a crook, and a liar. He returned from the Keys to fire his friend, hire me back, and then went back to the Keys.

After moving to Cobb County the first time, the stock experience I gained from my own investing, and the information I gleaned from my time with the liquor store, led to me being recruited as a broker. I took over a brokerage office on Broad Street back in Rome, of all places. That's where there was an opening. I took it. We were back to a place I knew well. Stacie, who finished college and would go on to get her Masters and start work on her PhD, was teaching and we had no kids yet.

We built a modest 1300-square-foot ranch home in Rockmart, Georgia. It lasted about 2 years and Stacie missed the convenience of Marietta, in Cobb County. We moved back to Marietta and I worked as a broker for a while longer, before circumstances moved us on.

While a broker, I sold a lot of a particular product from an investment firm. They recruited me to sell more of that product to other brokers. I received some of the top sales training in the world. Florida, Alabama, and South Georgia were my territory and I booked myself solid, constantly on the move for weeks on end.

They could tell where I was on any given day, based on where the business was coming in. I could sell to people who said they were never going to work with this company, and I would sell them big.

I would sit two seats down from my boss's boss and he would ask my opinion. I looked him up once and saw that he had a net worth of 500 million dollars. I took over his son's territory as his son was moving up in the company.

His son and I were making calls in Naples, and attending a conference at which I was presenting. We were sharing a rental car and he had me drop him off at a vacation home he had. I dropped him off at the gate for the neighborhood because he didn't want me to come in. It bothered me that, in his eyes, I wasn't good enough to be seen within his circles.

For a while, Stacie and I lived separate lives. It was more important for me to have my name mentioned every time they had a call about sales. I needed to be the best, but I felt very alone. That wasn't going to be healthy for my marriage.

I then worked for my father-in-law's repair shops. That business was just getting by. He didn't need the business to make him money, as he already had millions. They were making about $25,000 a month. I brought that up to $150,000. He resented me being successful more than he wanted the money. During our busiest times, he'd pull the mechanics to bail hay on his property and leave me to scramble to get work done. He wanted me to fail for his own selfish reasons.

In 2010, we had a falling out. As I said earlier in the book, he had a secret life and I saw into the books, figuring out what he was doing. He was making moves to cut his wife out of their money, to leave her with nothing. The deal was going to be that she could live in the house, but she would own nothing, and subsequently my wife and our kids would be cut out, too. Then, he could move on with his mistress and her kids he had been supporting in secret.

One day he was following me out into a parking lot and literally poking me in the face, asking me what I was going to do about it. I wanted to hit him, but I didn't. I tried to keep my mouth shut, but once I started talking, I told him what I thought of him.

I made sure his wife found out about it. I secured money for my kids in the future.

He did leave and not long after moving in with his mistress, she moved out on him.

After that falling out, and leaving the repair business, I got involved with a Kid to Kid store that I eventually bought. It was a resale business for kids' clothes and toys. The woman who originally owned it picked the location because it was near her neighborhood. There was no anchor store, among other issues. They had a going-out-of-business sale and closed up.

I went in with a flashlight after I bought it, and before the power was back on. Despite all the downsides, I felt it was mine the moment I stepped inside. I was starting from the bottom, but I was out from under the thumb of others. There was enough product left to get started, and to restock. One of the things sitting there on the counter of this abandoned store was a polka-dotted jumper that had belonged to my daughter. I knew my wife did business there, trading in stuff the kids had outgrown, but I had no idea I would find that there when the store became mine. It meant something to me.

I got the store cheaper than the asking price and invested heavily to get it back up and running. If the store failed, we failed, and I would take my family down with me. I never made a fortune there, and some months I couldn't pay myself, but we got by. The business grew.

I found out what the first owners did, and I did things differently from that. I got good employees. One didn't work out and I fired her within the first week. I never liked firing people, even when it was absolutely right and required. Too much was at stake to keep bad people in the business.

I knew less than nothing when I started. I ran it from 2010 through 2016, when I sold it for a good bit more than I had paid for it. That overlapped the time I got into my Uptown Cheapskate resale stores.

My Uptown Cheapskate stores are through Base Camp Franchising, owned by the Sloan Family. I like their setup because it provides me the perfect platform to build my own success and create rewards from my hard work for all of us. They recognize and encourage success, as well.

In 2012, I bought my first Uptown Cheapskate location. I got my parents to do the construction. I scraped together the money to pay for the place in cash. With interest rates as low as they were, I should have just financed and avoided the cash crunch I got into later.

Financial stress can bring you down faster than anything personally and professionally. I've done well, since, and have opened additional locations. I'm looking to expand even farther. Corporate is happy with me and has me mentor other store owners through some of the rougher parts of the learning curve.

As I write this, my team is at the conference in Utah. We won best grand opening of the year. We got a Peak award for over 25% operating profit. Not many stores get that. We got the Elite award which a few stores get and the Summit award. We outperformed other stores that got awards, but they can't give all the hardware to one place, I understand.

My father-in-law, like others, made promises he didn't keep. He told me at one point that I would take over the repair shop one day. Getting out from under his reign was a better reward. Some of the mistakes I made early in running my own business came from coming out steaming from working for him. It was like getting a bad beat in poker and then it can affect your judgement on the next few hands because you're tilted. I did learn my lessons, though.

I made efforts to reconcile with him over the years, and even reached out to thank him for the things he did do for me.

While I was a broker, I inherited the furniture from another office. I tapped my father-in-law to help me move it. In exchange, I let him keep most of it.

Not that long ago, I was looking for a new desk for

my home office space. My ex-wife said that her father still had one of those big desks from that brokerage, just sitting in his warehouse. I said I didn't want to deal with him on it, but she asked me to call him. She said he was dying of kidney failure, and had reached a point they just couldn't do much more for him. He was skipping testing appointments for getting on the transplant list. She said he was acting like he thought he could just get over it, like a cold. I suspect alienating everyone in his life makes the prospect of getting through the complexity of a transplant seem overwhelming. He was trying to tie up loose ends and get rid of things he didn't need. For that reason, more than the desk, I reached out to him again.

He told me a story about some generosity he showed in giving the city a deal on some land. I knew from others that his account of his "charity" wasn't exactly what he said it was, but I didn't call him out on it.

We made arrangements for my stepdad to pick up the desk. I couldn't make it out there, but my stepdad went at the appointed time and then called me. My ex-father-in-law wanted to know when I was going to pay for the storage. Like a decade of rent?

I called him, but of course, he didn't answer. I told him he could hold the furniture in place of payment, which was the original deal. I told him that if he felt like, after all these years, I owed him anything, send me an invoice and I'll pay it. I basically gave him a blank check. I haven't heard from him, and probably never will.

There are easier ways to get a desk, for God's sake. He will die as he lived. His daughter is the only one left to talk to him, and she'll be the one who has to clean up the mess he leaves behind—a shadow, instead of a legacy.

At the last moment, he just couldn't do it. He couldn't be straightforward. He couldn't let go of hurts, real or imagined. He couldn't help himself, but to destroy any relationship or small opportunity for redemption he might have left. He simply cannot help but to burn his life down around him at every moment.

On paper, he was a "success" for most of his life, minus everything he lost in two relationships that blew up at his own hands and cost him so much. He will die with money and someone will have to liquidate and sell off everything he did not manage to destroy on his own.

If the sign above Carl Brock's bed read: Abused alcohol since he was twelve, then I imagine the one above Stacie's father's head would read: In the end, he still couldn't help himself.

I learned a lot from all these experiences—both good and bad. As I talk about legacy, it would be incomplete if I didn't spell out my path to financial success. It does connect to leaving a legacy bigger than the money we leave behind.

So, I'll break down my philosophy and approach to business and financial success, as it stands now, where I'm making my path work for me. It is built off a range of knowledge and experience from multiple industries. The big ideas can be applied to your own path, even if it varies widely from my own. And, to be clear, there are some best practices, but there are no magic answers. Certain principles stand true, but there is no guarantee of success just because you follow a formula that worked for someone else. There are moments that hinge on seizing opportunities at the right time, and in the right way, which balance to a degree on what others are doing at a certain moment. Unless I'm looking over your shoulder at those moments, I can't list pros and cons of those decisions with you. It's good to find people you trust who can serve that sounding-board role, but it's still up to you to identify your opportunities, act upon them, and to not squander them once you got them.

With all that disclaimer out of the way, here is what I learned and how I generally operate in this realm of my life:

You can make money for someone else or for yourself.

I discovered, over many broken promises and much reward going into other people's pockets, that I was putting a lot of my best work into other people's profits. Every business thrives on people willing to make the business a success for their employers. Nothing wrong with that. There does come a point, though, that you have to ask yourself if that arrangement still works for you. Have you learned enough to take the chance on yourself? Is your path leading you to work for your own reward now?

In retail, especially, you start over every day. Every day starts from zero. You have to make it back that day. You have to manage your staff and other resources to make it happen. You are only so many paychecks away from poverty. It's scary, and every business endeavor you take on for yourself is like this to a degree, but sometimes it is the next and most important move in your life.

I managed to get in on the front of a wave, with my industry with the resale market. I think this time, for this market, may well be an important footnote in business history people will study later. It was my path.

No one will ever work harder for you, or longer for you, than yourself. You'll have to surround yourself with good people, but there will be times you can only count on yourself. In some ways, that is what working for yourself is really about.

You spend your entire life going after certain goals. Make sure your goals are worthy, for you, your family, and your time.

Hire the right people, get them invested, and empower them to act in the best interests of both of you.

I have a great employee who has been doing a great job with us. She has taken on some of our marketing, and has been doing online videos for the stores. We're very fortunate to have her. She just suggested a function at Kennesaw State University that she thought might be a good idea for the store to get involved with. I immediately said yes, without even reading it. I told her to plan on doing that herself, with another employee, and I will pay any fees for the event and I'll pay for their time, as well.

Hold on before you accuse me of being bad at

business for diving in before I look. The fact that she is motivated enough to want to do something, or is thinking about the company's interests, is invaluable to me. It is more valuable than the event itself. The event has great potential for my business, with her heading it up, because she is the most invested she can possibly be in making that event a success for both of us. I want to pay for her to do that, even if it's not the most beneficial single day. But it could be, because she wants it to be. I'm smart enough to know that she's smart enough and motivated enough to have a great idea, either this time or the next. And I don't want to miss it because I neglected or squandered her personal investment into my success, or because I wasted the opportunity to empower her leading up to those great ideas.

Utilize others' intelligence, skills, and energy to advance your cause, whether they work for you, mentor you, or your interests happen to align. Especially utilize those with much higher IQs, or with stronger specific skills than yourself. Seek those people out, if you can identify them. Once you learn what to look for, you can spot those people in a crowd. And treat them like they are a gift, so you can hold onto them, and mutually benefit from their growth.

Even when people move on from me, or our paths part, I strive to keep some level of contact as frequently as I can. One day, you may need to reach out to these people you have identified. One might be in a position to literally save your life or your business. The respect and kindness you showed during their growth can benefit you both, again, from where they find themselves later. It's not about using people, but being there for each other at all professional stages of life. The right people are the best resource.

In the end, with people who work for you, you can only ever pay them well, or treat them well. Not every industry is good at both, but they should pick at least one. If you do both, you will have great people who are often loyal to you for life. It beats hiring and training someone new every time you turn around. If you neither pay well nor treat well, then you are going to constantly lose your best people, and the ones you do keep will be dejected, and rightfully disloyal. You will lose your best and, eventually, you'll likely lose your business. There is also no way your terrible attitude toward people won't bleed over into your personal life, driving your loved ones away, as well.

Other people's labor and gifts are lent to you. When that leads to success, share with them. If their hard work leads to success that they never get a taste of, there is no reason for them to give more than the minimum. If you say, well, I pay them and that should be enough, then you don't get it.

Buy-in is everything as to whether your people are working for your success or not, even when you aren't standing over them. It's not about getting them "on the hook.". It's about the reward of having them truly invested in your success because they see it as their success, in the way a base paycheck alone does not achieve. Do you truly care about their benefit? Because without their wholehearted contributions, you won't reach the full potential of your business.

Your time has the value you set for it. Spend time as carefully as you would any precious resource in your business.

I have a numeric value for my time. I'll keep that number to myself. You should have a value for your time, too. Let's say for the sake of this discussion that your value is 500 dollars per hour. We'll use this number as a placeholder to understand the idea of using your time as a valuable resource.

So, for this discussion, you and I value our time at 500 dollars, plus, an hour. That's not to say that we make that every hour of our lives, 24/7. It does mean that I know what my time is worth to me, and I treat my time like it has real value. Because it does. Every professional interaction, from phone calls, to business meetings, to stocking shelves, to negotiating deals, to everything, is calculated on that scale. The further an activity or interaction falls from that assessed value, the more I have to ask myself whether this pursuit holds enough value for my time and business. I don't send invoices for my phone calls, but I don't spend more hours than I have to on unworthy pursuits. People are depending on me for their livings. Maybe someone else needs to handle this for me, or maybe this path is best left behind for one that reaches the value of my time, for me and my business.

You have to decide what your time is worth, and maintain that value in how you conduct yourself. If you spend every hour of every day working on your business, but on activities not worth your time, you'll destroy your business, neglect yourself, and your family.

Negotiating for land for new locations takes a lot of time. It has to be done. The purpose of an agent, in my mind, is so you never have to spend your time banging your head against every wall except the ones you choose to. Far more can be achieved through a high-paid mouthpiece than direct negotiations, in many cases. On a smaller but broader scale, this is what good employees do for you, too. The work has to be done, but your hours are better spent on other things they can't do for you.

This is going to sound like an odd application of this principle, but this is why I don't spend time badmouthing the competition. When given the opportunity, brag on them. Encourage people to visit you and them both, so that they'll appreciate how much better you are. I have competitors who I know are sending their employees to us, and then having them drop bad reviews in among all our good ones. They'll even post on our Facebook page. What a waste of valuable time. It shows desperation and turns no profit. When I respond well to their messages, they just made me look good in front of our customers, and made me more money. Badmouthing my competition is not worth my estimated value for my time. It shouldn't be worth yours, either.

Informed, open-eyed gambles are better than blind leaps of faith.

I've spoken with people who went into my line of business with just their retirement funds, and hoped for the best. Others started without enough capital to cover the first months and years properly. That's blind faith and a bad gamble. Informed gambles are better.

I opened my first Uptown store in 2012. We hope to have 10 stores within the next 10 years. Currently, we are building store number 4 in total, but I currently own 4 territories, from Kennesaw, Georgia to Chattanooga, Tennessee. I hope to, one day soon, open a store in Rome, Georgia, too.

We're still early in this adventure, but we have a million dollars plus in gross sales 3 years in a row. Only 12 Uptown Cheapskate stores, nationwide, have achieved that. We've had double digit growth for 8 years. Only about 8 stores with the corporation have done it 3 years in a row

Traditional retail is lucky to command 2.5 times cost. We're at 3 to 5 times return and that number is going up. Traditional retail stores are closing locations by the tens of thousands across the country. Payless shoes just closed over 2000 stores. Gymboree is going out of business. Crazy 8 is going out of business. Sears is going out of business. Kmart is going out of business. JC Penny, Macy's, most mall-based retailers are all going away, sadly.

I have a plan to re-purpose all that empty mall space across the country, if anybody cares to listen. That's not for this book, though.

We're getting that market share left in the void. Tougher economic times result in more merchandise for resale stores like mine, as well as more customers. As online business hurts certain sectors of retail unable to adapt, that builds our market potential in a way that I don't believe big online retailers can take from us.

On paper, it might look like a good time to sell, but I'm expanding because of the informed gamble I'm making on my business. I wouldn't be surprised to see an acquisition offer from a bigger company, like ThredUp or Amazon, in the next 5 to 10 years.

I have been influenced by good people along my path who gave good advice, but you have to be careful about who is whispering in your ear. I tend to mimic the people I surround myself with, so I'm careful about who those people are and what counsel they are giving me. Their influence upon you can be good or bad, in terms of the choices and decisions you make.

Without leaping blind, you have to assess your own path for your best gamble on yourself.

A little "greed" can allow for a lot of generosity.

By taking care of yourself and your business, you can allow others to benefit from your success. You can be more generous when you aren't bad with your money. The two go hand-in-hand, as counter-intuitive as that sounds. I suppose I would say there is a key difference between a little smart "greed" and outright selfishness. If you have no instinct to protect your interests and your business, you will miss out on the opportunity to be in a position to really help your family and friends when they need it most. If you are selfish, you will destroy the relationships and connections you require in order to grow your business and to live a life worth living.

Greed built empires and civilizations, but I try not to be stingy. I try to be fair in all my dealings.

Ongoing saving, investing, and credit maintenance make the difference between success or failure during lean times.

Money isn't any good, if you can't stop yourself from burning through it. The smarter you save and invest, the more likely you are to survive when times get tough, which they will. They always do.

Along the path, what gets you to your goals will be your resources, education, and experience, among other things. You have to manage your credit, too, or you will find yourself in a strangling pinch in a hurry. Life becomes so much more difficult.

Start early and start now, with saving. Be aware of your debt to income ratio. Pay your bills on time. If you destroy your credit, your odds of success are drastically reduced. If you have damaged it, take the steps needed to repair it, even if it takes a long time to do so.

Refusing to give up may be the most important barrier between success and failure.

Changing course is fine and can lead to success, if done wisely and not constantly, but giving up is not okay. It doesn't build habits that lead to success.

You have to believe in yourself, find ways to get by, and don't give up on yourself, even when things haven't worked out for you. You do what you have to do to make it work when things look to be at their worst. We get stuck in our minds and our failure becomes a self-fulfilling prophecy. Success usually lies on the other side of that moment, when everyone else has given up. Sometimes it is far on the other side of it, but that is usually where it is found.

That temptation to start over is always there and you end up firebombing your success, over and over. If I had to pin down one key piece of my success, it would be that, though I was tempted to give up many times, and even sometimes thought I had, I never really did. Everything I have now, is on the other side of those paths of giving up I chose not to take in the end.

Don't neglect the people who are important to you, who love you, in life.

I had to add this one onto the end. It is the one area where the most successful people find their biggest failure. This is where people gain the world, but lose their souls. They gather wealth, but die alone and without a legacy worth more than the dollars others took, and the plaques with their names on them, like the most expensive tombstones.

When engaging in mind games, you should assume the stakes are always high. This is especially true with your personal life. These kinds of games work in certain business deals, but destroy marriages. Ultimatums work better in business than in your personal life. A business relationship may start with an ultimatum, but a personal relationship will end with one. You can part ways in business and come back months or years later to work together again. If you part ways with your spouse, there is usually no coming back. If you decide to be a parent later, when you have more time and are more successful, you may never repair the damage you cause. This is an example of how the toolbox that allows one to be successful in business, does not translate well to your personal and family life. You need a whole new box and a whole new set of tools you may have not developed over the years.

People will always say family is the most important thing, but do your actions testify to that being true? Do you offer your valuable 500 plus dollar hours to the people who should mean the most to you? If you give every hour to business and let your family fall apart, you will have nothing left once you start to achieve success. That neglect will be your legacy, instead. That destruction within your personal life will bleed over into your business life, instead. I've watched people burnout as they strove to make their business work because they had nothing else. Their lives came out from under them and many failed businesses came next.

I've had to start developing a whole new toolbox. My legacy probably will include my business successes, but if it does not include my wife and children, then it means nothing beyond the dividing up of assets after I am dust. I'm striving for a legacy more important than the one corporate is giving out awards for. That's what the next couple chapters are about.

CHAPTER 7:

IN THE RING WITH ME

I REMEMBER MY first moment of real, overpowering, rage. I was five years old and still living in Kentucky. A neighbor kid had embarrassed me. I don't even remember what was done to me, but to this day, I remember the seething rage burning in my gut. I didn't know the word for it at the time, but in my core, I wanted retribution. I needed a release from that rage poisoning me from the inside. I could feel it burning me away to nothing. I started looking for a rope so I could hang that kid. I don't remember the resolution, but I'm sure the feeling eventually left me. I wasn't able to find a rope, and I never really found a good release for my anger for many years to come. I stepped into the ring when I was a kid, and never really stepped out again. Always raising my fists for the next round and the next and the next ...

Coaches of professional fighters often say to not fight angry. That's mixed advice. Having a little fire in a fight can drive a person to push through pain and exhaustion to win. But rage can lead to mistakes. It can cause a fighter to abandon the strategy and forget the game plan. It will cause them to lose patience and not work the fight properly, not waiting for the right openings, throughout the fight. Rage is a wildfire that burns up its source, and everything around it.

Many people over the course of my life have stepped into the ring with me out of anger, hate, and revenge. I usually welcomed every round because I wanted to hurt them and, sometimes, I wanted to punish myself. My family has been patient with me. Some have given up after enough injury. My parents worry about me, but they know they can't worry about me to me. People in my life tend to circle the edge of the ring without stepping through the ropes. They watch for openings to address issues or concerns, but they stay carefully out of range of my reach because my fists are always balled. There is no desire, nor incentive, for them to engage.

My wife Mendy is different. She is the only person who has ever stepped into the ring with me because she loves me. Because of that, I realize no one in my life has ever loved me the way she does. No one outside of my immediate family has ever tried as hard as she has to help me step out of the ring. Anyone else who tries gets to go home and rest up afterward. Mendy steps in with me, and then she has to stay with me for late rounds, too.

Mendy refuses to get angry with me. She puts out the fire with her love. I have been throwing everything I could find in my life on that fire, but nothing else has worked. I make it hard for her to fight for me. I know that I have made her feel like her feelings and her pain don't matter. It's time for that to change.

No one has loved me like her, and I want to do better at loving her like no one else has. I want to become what she needs me to be because I realize more and more, that is the man I am meant to be.

I met Mendy back in high school. We were in advanced chorus together and she sat behind me. We shared a mutual friend, but we weren't close. She dated a bad guy that I had some unfriendly interactions with. From my perspective, she was obsessed with him. I had a stronger opinion about him than I did about her, at that time.

She went to Shorter, too, but finished her time there a year before I arrived. That fact probably saved her some potential trouble.

When her daughter was still young, Mendy asked her first husband to leave. He was a bit of a conman, always working on a scheme. And really not much of a success at being a conman, at that. She wouldn't see him for days at a time and he was always running a racket. Her daughter wasn't but about two years old at the time, but Mendy recognized having him in their lives was never going to be anything positive.

It was just her and her daughter for a number of years before I came along

Mendy attended the same church as my mother, so I heard her name in passing a few times. I was at the church a few years back and she caught my eye. We started talking and she introduced me to her daughter.

I was dating a couple other girls at the time, but I started talking on the phone with Mendy.

She didn't realize our first date was a date. I invited her to Adretti's. She brought her daughter along and we played a bunch of games. We had a good time and I loved spending time with them.

HOW TO MAKE NO FRIENDS EVERYWHERE

Her daughter later asked her, "Why did you bring me along on your first date?"

Mendy laughed and said, "Oh, was that a date? You think so?"

We were on the phone together for hours at night, many nights. I bought the house I live in to be close to my kids. I was alone in that house. I had no pictures on the wall. The furniture at the time was just makeshift and utilitarian. I borrowed a couch from my parents and didn't much care about "making the place a home" for just me. I couldn't have felt more alone, and she filled a void no one else did.

I wanted Mendy to move in with me. We had only been dating seven or eight months before we decided to get married. It was decided over the course of several conversations. I needed her in my life, and still do.

I told one pretty damning story in a previous chapter about the last time I got drunk. For there to be a last time, there had to be other times. We had only been married a short period of time when she and I took a trip to Mexico. As happens when I try to drink socially, in a situation where it is hard to keep track of how many I've had, I got drunk. I got drunk enough to where I had a blackout and only remember bits and pieces. I get loud and mean, but I've never threatened violence against Mendy or anyone I've dated. For some reason, that line is hardwired into me, even when I'm at my worst. I'm thankful for that much.

I did leave Mendy terrified, though. She was crying because of how I was acting. I don't remember what I said, but I had her thinking I was ready to pack up and leave her, right there in Mexico. I behaved the same way on other occasions, acting like I wanted to push her away for being a stable force in my life wired for chaos.

That kind of behavior leaves a woman feeling like there is no security and no future. It only takes once for a guy to make someone he cares about feel that way, but it never happens just once. There is a key difference in relationships for men and women that men seldom consider. Unless you are dating someone who is crazy, most men never think about having to fight a woman. It doesn't cross our minds as a threat. We probably worry more about being struck by lightning. For women, it is different. A man raises his voice and he is just talking loud from his point of view. After it is over, he didn't do anything wrong. Just talked loudly. Women often think about having to defend themselves against men over the course of their lives. They think about it when they are out at night. They are told to be aware whenever they go anywhere in public. Any strange man who is approaching them along a sidewalk, following along behind them, or through a hallway in a public building, could be a threat. Men typically don't have a daily equivalent to this experience. When a man raises his voice, or shows signs of losing his emotional control, even if he has never been violent, the women present for this display have had to think about defending themselves against men many times before the shouting started this time. When a guy gives a woman he is dating or married to a reason not to trust him, he may slip into that same category of guys she had to consider as possible threats in the past. That's damaged trust that has to be repaired now. Men seldom think about that.

A while back I stormed out of the house at three in the morning. I didn't say I wanted a divorce, but I had made it clear I didn't care if she was there when I got back. When I got back, I actually expected her to be gone. She was still there. Unless I forced her out, she wasn't giving up on us. She is more than I deserve. She, and her attitude about not letting go of our marriage, is the only chance I have at success. She's got it together and has had to wait on me to catch up.

I found out later she had checked in with her mom to see if she could stay if I did force her out. She wasn't employed at the time. I was giving her no security and no reason to trust me. For a while, I was giving her no reason to love me, but she did anyway.

She figured out to let me fight myself, until I defeated myself. Instead of engaging in the pointless fight, she waited until I beat myself down. She came back in, surveyed the landscape, and stepped back in to let me know she still loved me.

My way of dealing with things was to pout a lot. I isolated myself. I played the victim a lot. Complained a lot. I was good at finding fault with everyone, and everything, other than myself. It forced people around me, and especially Mendy, to do a lot of gauging, reading, and walking on eggshells to navigate our relationship. If I've learned nothing else during that time, I've learned who I don't want to be.

I always knew she was smart. I knew she was strong, and has fight in her still, even after years of dealing with me. I can't watch *Jeopardy!* with her because she can run the board on her own. I always liked to believe I was two moves ahead as I advanced in business. I'm starting to realize just how wise, intelligent, and kind she really is, as she managed me all these years. And when I finally was ready to listen, she was ready with the solutions I needed, that she had been trying to tell me for a long time.

I knew she loved me, but I never appreciated just how much, until recently. I knew she had to bite her tongue at her own expense because of me. When my health started to break me down and forced me to stop indulging anger and rage so much, she was still here, waiting patiently to take care of me. I realized she had stepped through the ropes into the ring with me until I was done fighting everyone and everything. She was the only one who could outlast me, and wait for me to be ready to finally step out of those endless rounds of fighting for good. She broke down my barriers.

We are in the early stages of a changing dynamic now. I don't trust myself to not make more mistakes, or to not backslide. But I'm tired of hurting myself and others. I'm tired of being haunted by ghosts I keep alive. The biggest difference, now, is that I actually want what is best. I want to stop being at home in chaos and to start honoring what is good in my life and my family.

It had to start with small things. I accepted her advice on things and found it to work. I allowed her to love me, instead of constantly pushing her away. I started consulting her concerning things that impact us—including her in the process, instead of going my own way and expecting her to come along. I'm trying, anyway. I'm making a conscious effort to show her affection. I know that probably comes natural to many people in a loving relationship, but it is a set of muscles I'm having to build back after years of neglect, going back long before I knew Mendy. I'm willing to put in the work to make those things strong in our lives. I've been off by myself with work, with writing this book, and in dealing with pain and illness. I've chosen to move out of the office space by myself more often, to the level of the house she is on, so she doesn't feel alone. It's a change in physical location to put us on the same level, but it is part of a bigger effort to get us on the same level emotionally, mentally, and spiritually, as well.

Mendy's security, for so much of her life, was with her dad. When he died of cancer almost ten years ago, I believe part of her has felt adrift ever since. For the good of herself and her daughter, she had to send her first husband away, so she was a single mother for almost all of her daughter's life. She did a bang up job of it, in my opinion. Better than many two person teams I know. Better than I've done, up to now. But part of her life has remained off-balance since her father was taken from her. I wish to God I had tried to be a better balance for her before now. Now is what I got, though, so now is when I need to begin to set that right.

We were looking at some old pictures my mom brought over. Mendy got quiet and sad. She stepped off to herself and stared into the distance. My normal reaction would have been to leave her alone, because that's what I want when I isolate myself. I tried to make a better choice as her husband this time. I went to her and put my arm around her. I'm not trying to argue that I'm in line for some great husband award for this, but I'm pointing out that I'm going against my selfish and self-centered instincts to try to be what she needs me to be as her husband. Because I love her so much. Because I want her to experience how much I really love her.

She has cared so much for me when I wasn't well, and I want to start catering to her in equal measure. I've been here, but I haven't been present for so long. I hope I have caught the damage in time for healing. The structure under us has been compromised. I want to get out my new box of tools to stabilize, and to rebuild, our foundation.

She has been made to carry a tremendous amount of pain. She wants to be the best mother. She has been a great wife, above and beyond the call. Beyond what I deserved.

When I was a kid, I hid in an older cousin's trailer to try to escape my father. That cousin was Larry Brock, and his wife's name is Vonda. Once, when I was still young, I heard Vonda teaching something to her kids. The lesson wasn't intended for me, but I was listening in, anyway. She told them, "When you have done something wrong, you say, please, forgive me." Somehow, though I failed to apply that lesson so many times in my life, it got into my head and past the rage, into my soul. I said it myself when I got saved at Vacation Bible School in Kentucky. I've said it a few other times in my life, to both God and man.

Mendy, please, forgive me.

I love you. I adore you for loving me when I didn't deserve it. I am grateful for all the care, kindness, patience, forgiveness, and sacrifice you have shown me. I am still here, and capable of change, because you stepped into the ring with me and refused to give up on me. You still see the potential in me, and I am ready to strive to reach that potential. I believe I can be better because you are best. Please, forgive me for all the time I wasn't even good.

If there is one tool from my business toolbox that can apply to my relationships toolbox, it is the tool of never giving up. Mendy has been using that one on me for a long time. Now, it is time for me to be the husband she has needed me to be, and the one she deserves.

I started this book because I thought I might be dying. I was afraid I wasn't going to be here to explain any of this to my kids. I feared that I was going to leave behind shadows, instead of a worthy legacy. That's not the kind of thing you can fix in a few chapters of a book, but I wanted to, at the very least, give a history to explain where I fell short and how we got here—for better or for worse. I wasn't interested in excuses, but I did want my life to be recorded so they could understand me as much as possible. So they could know me better, if I wasn't here any longer. If I didn't have time to make it all right, I was going to do what I could to make it less wrong.

I started the book because I might have been dying; I'm finishing it because I might be living.

What does being married to Brent Brock mean? I know what it has meant, and that's not good enough. What does it mean going forward? If I can do well enough, with my loving wife's help, to make whatever years I have left good enough that these better years, these redeemed and reclaimed years, outshine the earlier years, that would be a blessing. As long as the years that I wrote about in this book don't overshadow what is ahead, then I will finally be the kind of success I need to be, in the areas of my life that mean the most. That would be a legacy. That would be a redemption story that would close off these pages nicely.

I love you, Mendy. Thank you for always loving me better than anyone ever has. I'm ready to step out of the ring, finally, to heal finally, and walk together into our future, finally.

CHAPTER 8:

IN OUR FATHERS' WAKE

BEING A FATHER may be the best scary thing that has ever happened to me. Nothing has turned my life over as fully, quickly, and completely, as having kids. I can't even explain how much I love them. I love my kids so much that I am thankful I had a brain tumor in 2007 because it indirectly led to them being born.

I'm going to dive into my health saga in the next chapter, but everything I have gone through, all the torment of surgeries upon surgeries, were worth it, if it brought my kids into my life, and if the pain and suffering from my health leads to me reevaluating my priorities to be a better man.

I wish I was smart enough, wise enough, brave enough, the right kind of strong enough, or listened well enough to learn my lessons easier. I wish there was a way to learn the lessons that suffering teaches, without having to suffer. Laying this story out on the page has let me know there is no other way for life, God, or the universe, to get through to me sometimes.

Stacie and I were trying to have kids after we were married and, like many couples, it wasn't happening for us. As things grew cold between us, and I struggled with drinking, there wasn't as much incentive to build a family together. After our first separation ended and I got sober, things got better between us for a while.

I was still distant, and we were not doing well leading into 2007, when I had to have a brain tumor removed. After that, I had the surgery described in the introduction of this book and we were still on shaky ground.

After the health scares and struggles we went through, Stacie softened on me and we started to think bigger than ourselves again. She said she wanted to try fertility treatments to have children. If I could have remained healthy, independent, and without the need of others, I'd have probably continued to pull away from her at a steady pace, instead. Thank God for brain tumors and internal bleeding, right?

Through the process of fertility treatments, we ended up with multiple attached embryos, and as the pregnancy unfolded, we ended up with twins making it to term. Once that news was certain, we shared the surprise of our coming twins with friends and family.

My ex-wife's father messed me up in a lot of ways over the years. The moment of sharing our wonderful news was no different.

He said, "Well, now you got two of everything. Twice the work and twice the cost. You'll need two bikes, two cars, two college tuitions, both at the same time … Just hope it's not a boy and a girl. They won't be able to share as much then."

We had a boy and a girl.

Becoming a father was the best and worst thing. It was the best because of who my kids are and who they are becoming. God, I wanted to do right by them, and still do. It was the worst because I was ill-prepared for fatherhood. Every man is, but I had gathered extra ghosts to keep my head full of trouble. This pull between the best and worst inside me explains the need for this book to come out of me, more than anything.

I was scared for so many reasons. My past, and my financial concerns. I was in a panic. My father-in-law had gotten into my head again at the worst time.

I stayed home with the kids for the first few months so Stacie could get back to work. Once they were a little older, she felt better about other people watching them.

I wanted to do anything in my power to make them not turn out like me. Being a parent for me is so much about basic survival, sometimes. Having some grand strategy to build them into people who transcend their family name is a tall order for anyone. They are becoming wonderful people, but I have trouble giving myself credit for any of that.

When they were five, Stacie and I split up for the last time and divorced. It wasn't a good situation. They witnessed us arguing. They saw mom and dad being cold to one another. As I struggled through my own anxiety and isolation, we tried our best to shield the kids. We kept them in a separate part of the house when I was in a mood, and closed in the bedroom. The kids stayed with grandma while we were working through things. Or not working through things. I screamed in my son's face about something and made him cry. I imagine he still remembers that. I know I do. It sticks with me.

We sat them on the couch and explained to them how mommy and daddy were not getting along, how we still loved them, and how we were going to be parents for them, while not all living together. Do you ever really explain that sort of thing well enough for kids who are about to have their troubled home completely broken? We barely understood what we were doing, ourselves, and we were supposed to be the adults in the family.

We worked out joint custody. We set up my weekend and my weekday and alternating holidays. We were flexible, and I stepped in whenever Stacie needed me. I've always gotten them more days than what was laid out in the agreement. Never as much as I want to see them, but that is not Stacie's fault. If we couldn't live together, then I can't see them every day, and we simply couldn't live together. We used the same attorney and worked out the details. Using the same attorney is generally a bad idea with any case, but we pulled it off. We cared about the kids more than ourselves, and that was good.

When I was still living with my friend, I had the kids over there and he'd make himself scarce, so we had the house to ourselves. We'd camp out in the living room. I've always fought the temptation to just be the fun dad. That would be easy to pull off with an every-other-weekend situation. I want them to grow up to be good people, so I work hard to not spoil them, and to maintain discipline while I have them.

I moved into an apartment, eventually. Stacie sold the house we used to live in and bought another. I wanted to live near my kids, so I bought a house 5.2 miles down the road. I didn't want to live right next door to my ex-wife, but I wanted to be convenient to their lives.

My biggest difficulty with trying to be a good father is the fact that it is me trying to do it. Everywhere I go, I have to bring me along. My personality, and way of conducting my personal life, has always required others to develop their habits around me, to accommodate me. That has been the experience for my kids, as well, to some degree as they have grown up. They are ten now as I am writing this, and my son has fallen into line with that unfortunate dynamic more than my daughter. I'm trying to unwind that, so that being my child does not require bending their lives so much to suit me.

We went to a play recently with Mendy, Mendy's daughter (currently 15), my twins, myself, and Mendy's daughter's boyfriend. I don't think it is any guarded secret that I'm not a fan of the guy. Maybe I see the worst in guys because of what kind of guy I was. Maybe I have a nose for trouble, because of the kind of guy I was. It could be that I'm not going to like any guy the girls date, but I don't think that's exactly it. The guy has lied to me, and has a couple other habits I read as disrespectful. I wouldn't be doing my job, if I didn't keep an eye on him.

I was irritable about the seating arrangement, and a few other details of the night. I discussed it quietly with Mendy as we were settling in. My daughter is good about eavesdropping, but not great at disguising it. I told her to stop spying so I could finish my conversation.

As I settled down and settled in, I leaned over and got both my kids' attention. I told them, "Listen, you guys haven't done anything wrong tonight, and everything is okay. I'm sorry if I'm being negative. Don't let my negative energy become yours."

I'm trying to do better about being a secure, stable, and loving presence in their lives. I'm checking in with them more. I'm trying to read them better to be sure they are okay. My daughter is opening up more.

My son was going through something recently that had him in a quiet mood. I checked to be sure he was okay, but didn't force him to tell me anything. The only message I wanted to get across was that I loved him, and I was here for them.

I'm trying to give them what I knew was missing for me, sometimes. Early on, if someone had told me that I hadn't done anything wrong when things were in chaos, or when we were in danger, or when we were pulling up roots so often, that would have meant a lot. There would have been the potential for an emotional foundation that I feel like I lacked from being unsettled through so much of my early development.

My kids are both bright. Much brighter than myself. We made sure to immerse them in education. Their mom is in advanced levels of her own education. We played them Beethoven and Bach in the womb. Did it work? I'm not sure, but my son is in 4th grade, working on a high school vocabulary level. I challenged him to teach himself Spanish from YouTube. They both read, and pick up on so much so quickly.

I'm torn between the ideas of giving them all the best in life, and preparing them to be resilient. As I write this book, I'm innately aware of how different our childhoods were. We almost grew up on different planets. I lived as a nomad, while they have deep roots at age ten.

We live in a 6-bedroom, 4,000-square-foot home. We have large green spaces—two parks and three playgrounds. Several tennis courts, a clubhouse, and a neighborhood pool are available. The pool is available year-round, enclosed, with heat in the winter. We have a large turtle pond and fishing pond. There are walking trails and well-lit, paved, running trails. We have the nearby convenience of suburban living, but a feeling of being in the country. When we have incidents in the area, detectives are dispatched. The chairman of the Cobb County School Board is my neighbor. I know many of the business owners in our area. I feel respected in our community. My kids attend one of the best public schools in the nation.

All of that is important, but all of it matters less if I don't step up to be the kind of father I know they need me to be. Roots don't thrive if they are not nurtured. There are so many ways to parent wrong. I don't expect to be perfect at anything, even under ideal circumstances, but I know I can do better than how I have done in so many areas.

When Mendy and I started dating, she and her daughter lived in a modest home, in a diverse neighborhood. They were both super-nerds about Disney and Harry Potter, among other things. Mendy tried to take her daughter to Disney about once a year. They found out I hadn't seen the Harry Potter movies, so we watched them all.

As we got more serious, I pulled Mendy's daughter

aside and discussed the possibility that Mendy and I might get married. The response was immediate. Mendy's daughter said flatly, "No, it's always just been the two of us."

Of course, we did get married, but that was the barrier set, that I had to get over.

We had Mendy's daughter's thirteenth birthday. I rented out a space at Dave and Busters for her and her friends. It turned out to be her first real party. Mendy took great care of her daughter, but her daughter was a little embarrassed to have friends over, so they had always gone with just family on birthdays. I understand that feeling. It made me think back to my first real party at the McDonald's. I'm glad that her experience with the party was better than mine.

Mendy's daughter wants nothing to do with her biological father, even in the rare moments that he wants to connect with her. She was maybe two when he left, so I'm not sure she has any real memory of him. She doesn't take his calls. So, from then on, her only male influences have been her grandfather and her uncle, Mendy's father and brother, until I showed up. After Mendy's father died when her daughter was 5, that took something important away from both of them.

Back in high school, a random series of events resulted in me being at the house when Mendy's dad was there. I remember her father because of that random night. I remember Carl Brock beating on a trailer, threatening to kill me, and talking about going fishing, on his deathbed. Mendy tells of remembering her father as he looked when he was standing at the top of the stairs. I can picture it, because I saw it that night. Both men left a wake behind them through their lives, and we still feel those waves today.

Her father stands as an imposing, but not a threatening, figure at the top of those stairs. He left a legacy, but not the kind of shadow Carl Brock did, or that I fear I still might. Mendy's father had his own version of a C.S. Lewis quote that she shared with me as the ten year anniversary of his passing is upon us. "Strength isn't how much you carry, but how long you carry it. And strength is also about knowing when to stop carrying it." I'm trying to develop that type of wise and enduring strength. And to leave that kind of legacy for my kids.

My relationship with Mendy's daughter has been slow to develop.

As of the time I am writing this, her 15th birthday was last week. We were having the whole family meet at Longhorn Steakhouse to eat. It turned into a big confusing mess, at first, because I was on the phone with my mom trying to figure out where she was in the restaurant. I ran into people I knew and had to talk to them for a moment. Eventually, I figured out that they were at a different Longhorn, 25 minutes away.

I stepped back into the alcove where the hallway to the bathrooms were, so I could hear her and work things out. Mendy and her daughter were still searching the restaurant. I decided to have my parents and the family save us a seat. I said we could call back once we were on our way, and they could place our order. Our food would get there as we got there, and we could all eat together.

My stepdad, Junior, thinks a lot like me. He

wanted to go with the least complicated solution. I believe Junior is a gift to me from God, because he is one of the few people in my life who doesn't just bend to my will. He said, why don't they eat there, and we eat here, and we can meet up another time.

Normally, that would be the way I would go, too, but there were other things more important than simplicity. I got a little hot about it, because I was frustrated. I didn't explode like I might normally do, but I said, "No. No. I'm not having my daughter's birthday at two different restaurants. We are coming there to all eat together as a family."

I looked up from the corner where I was standing, and saw Mendy and her daughter. I met eyes with them and my fifteen-year-old daughter kind of looked away. I realized that was the first time I had called her my daughter, that I recall. Almost definitely the first time she had heard it from me. I had always been careful not to presume anything as I became part of their family, which had always been the two of them. In truth, we were a family long before that was said in a frustrating mix-up at the Longhorn, but I'm glad it was said and heard, because it is the truth.

My fifteen-year-old daughter is wicked smart. I feel that way about all three of my kids, and I'm sure I am biased, but the evidence is pretty strong. My fifteen-year-old hides it well. She doesn't have to study to make As and Bs. I suspect she, herself, doesn't realize how smart and talented she is. I think she doesn't know how to focus it, and sometimes that paralyzes her.

My fifteen-year-old was out with her boyfriend, and came home after curfew. It was raining and I was standing out on the porch waiting when they pulled up. She was supposed to have been one place, but she was at another with her boyfriend. The vehicle pulled up at an angle to the driveway. Our daughter got out and I could tell whoever was driving, it turned out to be her boyfriend's nineteen-year-old sister, was debating whether to get out or not. I expected her boyfriend to walk her to the door through the rain, but she came alone.

After she was almost there, he finally stepped out. This wasn't the only thing that set me off. The guy didn't open doors for her, even though I've seen her open a door for him. I told her later not to serve any guy like that, who wasn't serving her. He let his mother call us to ask about seeing our daughter on a couple different occasions, instead of calling for himself. He doesn't answer with "sir," nor does he show other basic respect that makes me suspect what he is like when no one is around.

So, he stepped out of the car after all that, and after she was almost to the house, and I told him, "Get your ass back in that car. I want to talk to the adult driving."

Our daughter stopped short of the porch. She thought I was talking to her when I said that. I said to her, "Go upstairs and wait for me and your mother."

She went without complaint, which surprised me a little. She's not a bad kid at all, but I thought this might be a moment of rebellion, but she didn't play it that way.

She went upstairs and he got back in the car. The brake lights came on for seven seconds and then went off. The car drove off without any adult getting out, which told me there wasn't one in the car.

Mendy and I went to her room. I told her, "We're going to play a game. The rules are, we can't lie to each other. You can say you don't want to answer. You can say we don't want to hear the answer. But we don't lie."

She agreed and she told the truth. We had a discussion about a series of bad choices. We discussed inexperienced drivers in the rain. We discussed punishment for not being where she was supposed to be.

I had a blank check when I was a kid. I'd get in trouble with the police and then my stepdad would badmouth the dirty crooked pigs with me on the way home. I'd go where I wanted to go, and they wouldn't know where I was until I sent a postcard from another country, sometimes. That didn't produce the best results. I don't want to leave my kids to destroy themselves, and I don't want to be anything like the monster Carl Brock was.

One thing I want them to know for sure, is that I support them with whoever they turn out to be. I don't want them to listen to, or to conform to, anyone who tells them to be less than who they really are. No one else gets the right or power to define them.

Our fifteen-year-old was a little standoffish with my twins when we first blended our families. The twins were excited to have an older sister, but our older daughter was overwhelmed with all the new family, wanting time to herself. It was a little hard on my kids.

Recently, Mendy bought a ball for the twins to play with while they were over. She came to me and told me that my ten-year-old daughter was a little upset. My son was playing with the fifteen-year-old, and my other daughter felt left out. I was kind of happy. Not because my younger daughter felt bad, but because they were initiating with each other as siblings in the same family. That's a good moment. That's progress.

I used to think people were a bad influence on me. I thought others brought out the worst in me. There's more evidence that I was the bad influence on others.

I had already seen some ugly stuff while I was still very young. But I didn't have to do the things I did; I chose to.

I'm sure my name has come up in counseling sessions with a number of people. I left a lot of trauma in my wake, for a lot of people. Sadly, that was me being controlled. There was far darker potential through all those years.

I used to think being bad took courage. Bucking the system and defying expectations, to do what I wanted to do and nothing else. Walking into a group of girls and being funny was my height of courage, when I was young. Getting beer for the party was courageous. Fighting anyone, for any reason, was strength. Talking myself out of the consequences of my actions was my version of wisdom.

Being me is harder than it should be. Do I have what it takes to make it easier to be in my life, and to love me? Do I have that kind of courage in me?

Being a better husband and father is the hardest thing I've tried to do in my life. I've not been successful at that for extended periods of time.

So, if I'm here for twenty more years, what does that look like? What legacy will that leave behind?

Where do I go from here? How do I change the waves in my wake?

I think of my memories up until I was ten years old, and it leaves me a little cold. I had trouble getting hold of my own mind. I didn't know who I was, or where I was going. I didn't like myself or my life. I didn't understand anything that was going on. Maybe at 47 I can start to get a handle on some of those things. Maybe I can show that kind of courage.

I know my children's memories up to this age are worlds different from mine, but that does not excuse me from being a better father figure going forward. I need to be more loving, humble, and present, as a father and as a husband. They need to see the love I have for Mendy to know what they should be looking for in life and in love, in the future. They need to see me become the kind of person they can strive to be. I don't want to leave any more damage in my wake. I want to leave them with a legacy that empowers them, even after I am gone, instead of a shadow that haunts them.

Strength isn't how much you carry, but how long you carry it. Strength is also knowing when to stop carrying it. It's time for me to become the right kind of brave and strong.

CHAPTER 9:

I'M NOT MUCH, BUT I'M ALL I THINK ABOUT

EONS FROM NOW, when future archeologists dig up my grave, they may find a little bone dust and they will also find several pieces of surgical mesh which did their very best to kill me, despite all the promises doctors ever made to me. If that is all the evidence that is left of me when this civilization becomes ancient, it will tell an important part of my story, and be evidence of my suffering.

I've had chronic stomach issues for as long as I can remember. As a kid, I'd be in the car on the way home from eating somewhere, in the fetal position with my knees in my chest. It would torture me for days or weeks at a time. Other times, I might go months or even years without an episode. But it never stopped completely.

I've also lived with near-uninterrupted stress in my life. Sometimes it was of my own making, and sometimes it was social-environmental. I did my fair share of finding ways to make the physical, mental, and emotional stress in my life worse. The amount of rough mileage I've put on my life is now documented in this book. When I was in high school, I was already joking that I was taking years off my life. Not as funny once you find yourself in the late miles of the journey.

I've always been in fight-or-flight mode. That hyper-vigilance will tear a person apart, inside and out. It has become my natural state and my body is not cooperating anymore. Whatever medical causes lie underneath my health issues, this state of ever-present stress can only hurt.

We started this book with the story of me fighting a brain tumor and then nearly bleeding to death, from the inside, before a rushed surgery. Then, I woke up too soon and they had to hold me down to keep me from ripping my stitches. I have come to suspect that some of my nurses handling me during that 2007 stay, may have exacerbated the situation getting me up in bed one time. There is a lot of potential blame to go around as we move forward with this chapter.

My kids were born in 2008, but while Stacie was pregnant, I was diagnosed with an abdominal hernia, specifically an incisional hernia, from that 2007 episode. Whatever the primary and secondary causes of the complication, it resulted in the incision being pulled apart on the inside, which can't be healed—not when it is the internal incision that splits. When that happens, you're stuck with it.

I could see the bulge of intestine coming out of the abdominal wall. It was unlikely to get pinched, but was possible, and could result in perforation and death.

My doctor suggested this new medical mesh that could be used to tack it together. It was supposed to be revolutionary. It would stretch and contract with weight loss, weight gain, exercise, and everything.

It was new. It had just come through testing.

I asked, "How good is it?"

My doctor answered, "It is so good, when archeologists dig up your grave ..."

Sounded great. Where do I sign?

It broke a year later. I was running at the time and it was a nightmare of pain.

In 2009, I found a specialist at Emory. There was no greater authority that I could find, anywhere. When he went in, he discovered the mesh had become a part of my body. They would have to cut it out to a degree that would kill me. I was stuck with this garbage product forever. He ended up having to add more to reinforce what was already there.

It wasn't his first choice for a solution, but he assured me I would never have a problem again. I reminded him of the fact that he said that two years later, when I was back with more split mesh.

In 2011, we came up with another plan. They added implants to my body cavity to add girth to reinforce the damaged area and make it harder to break again. And they added more mesh. At this point, I had multiple versions of this product, from multiple manufacturers.

This was followed by tons of recalls and class action lawsuits. This stuff was ruining lives. It was breaking apart inside people. It migrates, tearing organs and killing people. I went around and around with lawyers who didn't think I had a case. That may have changed, but it is ongoing. I'd love to get an apology as part of any settlement. There is no amount of money that will give back what the makers of this stuff took from me, but I'd still like to see them pay, just the same.

I got discharged after yet another surgery. I got my first meal after coming off the liquid diet. It wasn't much, but I got violently ill. My mother held a pillow against my stomach while I got sick, to keep me from breaking my incision. This was 2012.

I ended up back in the hospital. My doctor told me, "I don't know what's going on. I don't want to go back in again. Let's give it some time and see if we can get it to heal."

That was the beginning of seven hard days. I had so much pain and so much anxiety.

My stomach did start working again. No one celebrates you passing gas like nurses in a hospital.

In the midst of all this, my doctor leaned down and whispered to me, where no one else could hear, "I think I nicked your bowel when I was operating on you. I thought if that was it, then it would heal up. And it did."

That was his diagnosis and confession.

No one could tell me why it kept happening. No one could come up with a root cause and cure for things that plagued me my whole life and kept happening. I just wanted people to come in and do their jobs. Stop all the hemming and hawing, figure out what it is, and fix it.

Since all this, I've tried not to pick things up beyond my medical weight limit. Even when the kids got too big, I stopped lifting them up.

Back in November, there was something in my vehicle that wasn't supposed to be there. It represented someone not doing their job, and I was stuck with it. That sort of stuff really pisses me off.

So, this big spool of cable wiring for security

cameras was in the back of my truck as the family was getting ready to pack for a trip. I put down the bags I was carrying and reached in to get it out. Mendy hurried to put down what she was carrying to keep me from having to do it, but I already had it in my arms at that point.

"Let me help you."

Words we should learn to accept in most every situation, no matter how independent we are, or how much pride we have.

I grabbed the spool in a bear-hug and hoisted the whole hundred plus pounds up on my chest and above my weight limit. She cleared off the table where I was going to put it in the garage while I stood there holding it.

I was trying to be calculating, keeping the weight off my stomach.

Symptoms started five days later. From there, it got worse and worse and worse ...

Because of my past trauma, I was reliving it all again as symptoms increased. My stress increased right along with them.

They couldn't go back in for another surgery. There was too much damage. Too much scar tissue. Too much that could go wrong, and not enough that could go right.

I internalized the fear. I knotted up my own gut more than my physical symptoms already had. It was becoming a self-fulfilling prophecy.

I took to bed for days and it got worse. I just stayed in the fetal position for days. Mendy noticed this pattern and later suggested that curling up in bed might be making it worse, based on what she saw. I was making it worse by staying rigid, both in and out of bed. She later suggested hot baths and other ideas that, once I listened, actually helped. That is recent, though. I wasn't seeing the patterns yet, and I wasn't listening to her. She had to wait until I was listening, God bless her.

The Mayo Clinic ruled out the mesh pretty early. So, we were back to old problems following me my whole life.

It got to where I couldn't even drink water without it getting worse. I really started to fear for my life. I couldn't eat; I couldn't drink. An old friend of mine, who is a brilliant doctor, suggested a rare condition that might be at the heart of it. I passed it on to my doctors at the Mayo Clinic to consider. My friend, as a doctor, was deeply concerned about how quickly I was losing weight. I had it to lose, but then I kept losing it beyond that point, too.

Mendy is stuck with me every day. That may be to her personal disadvantage, but it gave her a data collection advantage over the best doctors. She knows me. She's observed me. When I was ready to listen, she suggested things that have helped, partly because they help reduce stress and relax my rigid body to keep my systems moving. Partly it worked because she is brilliant, and I finally started to pay attention.

I thought I was dying. I thought it was imminent. Everything that has transpired during the process of writing this book grew from this. I wanted to find some redemption. I wanted to make atonement. I wanted to make sense of it all. I needed to understand, and if I could understand, finally, then maybe I could explain it in writing to the people I loved—the people I had failed to show and express the full measure of my love to, through all this pain, damage, and scar tissue. I didn't want to go back into my past emotionally and spiritually, and risk tearing open these old wounds, but I had to fix what was killing me and the people I loved.

This process has changed me in profound ways. I hope I am up for it. I hope I can move forward with it.

What suffering teaches us can sometimes not be learned any other way. Maybe I can share some of what I've learned and spare you a few unproductive rounds in the ring yourself.

You're not in this alone, even when you try to be.

Others depend on you, and they suffer when you suffer. They hurt for you because they care about you, so to think they are not a part of your suffering is maybe one of the worst forms of narcissism and selfishness. It is difficult to think of others when we are dealing with chronic pain and chronic illness. But those that love you feel a different kind of pain, because they want to make it better for you, but they can't, so sometimes the best they can do is to just be there for you and that means a lot. Others' lives are impacted by how you handle your difficult times.

You can't live life alone.

You may want to. You may even be able to fool

yourself into thinking you can. It is easier to believe we can live as an island when we are healthy. That illusion gets shattered when we are not well. But don't be fooled; it was an illusion the whole time. Your life is incomplete when lived alone. It does not mean you have to be dating someone or you have to be married, but you were not meant to face this life alone, or in isolation. It is better when you don't isolate.

You don't have to live alone.

To think we are truly alone often requires us to ignore those who are reaching out to help us at this very moment. We have to constantly push people away in order to be alone. Being alone is more of a choice than we realize, often times. If we seek people out, if we return to those who loved us, if we open our eyes to the people in our lives, we will be surprised how loved and included we can potentially be.

Pain enables empathy.

If you are in pain, real pain, over enough time, it becomes harder to ignore the pain of others. You start to recognize the signs, like you are sharing a secret, unspoken language between you and others who suffer. It becomes especially hard to ignore the pain that you have caused in others. You don't just sympathize with the hurt of others; you feel your pain again, and you empathize with them. It becomes harder and harder to see the flaws in others, because you are able to see their pain and suffering so much easier than before.

Suffering brings the past and the future into clearer focus.

At the same time that pain keeps you focused so tightly on the present, you are almost forced to consider the past and the future differently than when you are well and running on autopilot. You would think pain would make it hard to think about anything else, and it does. But when things are going along fine, your past and future will slip into the background. You may think about them, but only in the abstract way we do when death is the farthest thing from our minds. When you hurt enough to where death feels close, the past and future become more concrete. The pieces of the puzzle start to hold more meaning for you, because it could all be over. At that point, missing pieces become maddening. You have to understand who you are, and what it all means. Unfinished business and unresolved issues now need to be finished and need to be resolved.

The shadow of death narrows and sharpens your priorities.

Just as the closeness of death brings the past and future into focus, it also cuts away unworthy and unimportant priorities in a hurry. The things you worked the hardest for can be exposed for how unimportant they really were, compared to other things and people you neglected. Time feels short and there is only so much of it left to make it right.

Writing about the past and future reveals patterns of truth in your life.

If these lessons taught through suffering lead you to start writing about the past and future, well then, God help you. As you lay out your life, in whatever form you analyze it, you will see patterns you hid from yourself up until now. You start to see history repeating itself and then realize you're about to make the same mistakes all over again. Breaking the cycle becomes imperative.

The truth rings true and stings your pride.

I felt that sting a lot writing this book. That's usually when I knew I was onto something true. I felt it in my pride—that part of myself that wanted to stop telling the story, and the part that wanted to just go on like I always had, without having to change. The ring of truth is when one of the lines hit so close to home, that there was no denying it. It was like pulling back a curtain to finally see the light. It hurt my eyes more than hiding in the darkness, but I needed that light in order to see. Be thankful for any friend or loved one in your life who can tell you that kind of pride-stinging truth in a way that you'll finally hear it.

If all this leads me to be a better husband and father, I wouldn't trade any of it.

I can be a mean-spirited person. My life has been preparing me to be that way for a long time. It is my natural default, if I'm left to my own devices. Going through difficulty, and the health issues that have stopped me in my tracks over and over, have changed my outlook. It is natural for me to be mean, selfish, and hot-tempered, but that's not who I am, and it's not who I want to be. All of this has led me to re-evaluate my life, and has given me a chance to choose a different path. If I can switch paths now because of what I have gone through, then it was all worth it— every painful moment of tough lessons learned and relearned.

CONCLUSION:
FEELING THE LIFE COME BACK IN

CARL BROCK, my biological father, casts a wide shadow over my life, all the way from those haunted Appalachian hills of Kentucky. I sometimes believe that he experienced life backwards. He was sentenced to Hell at birth, and lived his life condemned before his death finally set him free. His passing should have set me free, too, but I wasn't the kind of strong where I knew when to stop carrying my burden.

God is love. That is what the Bible says, and I'm inclined to believe that short, clear, assertion. The absence of love leaves anger and hate, and those are the building blocks of Hell. I don't need a book to tell me that truth, because I've experienced it. It rings true and stings my pride. Carl Brock carried hate and anger around in his heart every day. In the absence of love, he carried his own little piece of Hell around inside him everywhere he went and, like Hell, it burned dark. He poured alcohol on that piece of Hell inside him, burning himself and every soul he came into contact with.

I'm striving to be better than all that. The man has been dead and buried for years. It's past time for his spirit to be cast out for good, too. I have a loving wife and three incredible children who deserve a place at my side, so I don't have room for a crooked bootlegger ghost anymore.

The introduction of this book opened with a moment where I brushed death. I felt the life drain out of me. The message that I got was that it was okay. I was out of control and I could do nothing to save myself, so it had to be okay.

Then, I felt the life come back into me. There was a lot of pain and suffering ahead of me. I was out of control and I could do nothing to save myself from it, but in time, it was going to be okay. God was not done with me. People who loved me were not going to be done with me. My journey wasn't, and still isn't, finished. And it's okay. Because life is possibility. Love is potential. And it's not done yet.

I felt the life pour out of me as I wrote this book. I bled out everything I had onto the pages. All my past, all my failures, all my pain, and everything that was me, was laid bare until I felt like my entire soul was emptied out. As I finished the last few chapters and shared them with the people I loved, and sometimes with strangers, I felt the life coming back into me. It's something new. It is all possibility and potential I don't want to waste.

Some of the words sting and ring for other people, too. The core of both fiction and, in the case of this book, nonfiction, is the truth. Does it tell the truth? Any character in any story, told in any format, only matters in so far that their story is true to that character. I have done many things wrong in my life, but what I feel like I got right in these pages, is that I told the truth. If it helps you, if it helps anyone, that will be why.

I'm at the beginning of something and I know that I have to bring myself along with me, despite all my history and flaws. Something is changing though and I'm excited to see what could happen.

I'm ready.

Ready to be more than my pain and my past.

I was camped out in hopelessness for a long time. Hopelessness is a lie, but I wasn't ready to hear the truth. My pain and my past got me here. They helped shape me. They have helped me come to the realization of the need to change. I'm not going to be limited to what my past and pain predict for my future. From here, I have the opportunity to transcend those things.

Ready to define myself, rather than being defined by other people and other things.

If you don't define yourself, others will do it for you. It is important to take an active role in your definition. It will inform your choices, your actions, and your future. That is too important to outsource to others.

Ready to extend my success into my personal life.

I've exceeded my own expectations of my success I

had when I was young. And I'm far from done. I need a different tool box for my relationships, though. It is time for me to start using those tools to build success where it matters the most.

Ready to demonstrate my love for my wife and children.

My wife and kids know I love them. I still need to reinforce that knowledge for them through my actions. They should be constantly reassured of the truth of my love for them. It should be consistently demonstrated, so they can draw strength from it all through their lives, even after I am dust and recalled medical mesh.

Ready for a legacy that is more than a list of successes and failures.

We all leave behind something. It is either a shadow or a legacy. I will leave behind money for my children. They deserve more than that, though. This book is part of that process of leaving them more. I need to nurture who they are, and who they are becoming. I want them to go beyond me, and exceed the example I set for them. I want to leave an example worth striving toward. I want my legacy for them to be something they can build off of, and that encourages them toward greatness. Both success and failure are good teachers, if we pay attention to the lessons being taught. Legacy is beyond those things. A legacy is a clear path forward, during and after our lives. It is bigger than us, and bigger than our short time here on Earth. But it has to be built during our lives. Use your life to build something good and true, that matters beyond your days.

ABOUT THE AUTHORS

BRENT BROCK

In this case, the entire book is about the author. Come check out Brent Brock's Uptown Cheapskate locations in Georgia in Acworth, Woodstock, and Kennesaw. More locations coming soon. Check out UptownCheapskate.com to locate the store nearest you. If you are interested in learning more about franchise opportunities for yourself, you can e-mail Brent at NoFriendsNoWhere@gmail.com or text UCACWORTH to 37727 for more information. He would love to help you see if owning your own business might be part of your path to success and a legacy as well.

JAY WILBURN

Jay Wilburn has ghostwritten a wide range of nonfiction, but this coauthored work is the first nonfiction release in his own name. He has work in *Best Horror of the Year volume 5* and has had stories nominated for awards. He is a kidney transplant recipient and is training for a double marathon, 52.4 miles. He is the author of the *Dead Song Legend* series, *The Enemy Held Near, A Yard Full of Bones,* the *Lake Scatter Wood Tales* series for young readers, and many more great stories. Support him on Patreon at Patreon.com/JayWilburn.

Made in the USA
Columbia, SC
25 May 2020